PROUD AMERICAN

The Migrant, Soldier, and Agent

J. MARCELLUS BURKE,

THANK YOU SO MUCH FOR
YOUR SERVICE TO OUR COUNTRY.

THE GREATNESS OF OUR DESTINATION IS
LOST WITHOUT THE MEMORY OF
OUR BEGINNING.

SERGIO A. TINOCO

6-23-2017

Proud American: The Migrant, Soldier, and Agent
Copyright © 2017 by Sergio A. Tinoco

Library of Congress Control Number: 2017942300
ISBN-13: Paperback: 978-1-64045-391-3
           PDF: 978-1-64045-392-0
           ePub: 978-1-64045-393-7
           Kindle: 978-1-64045-394-4
           Hardcover: 978-1-64045-515-3

Printed in the United States of America

LitFire LLC
1-800-511-9787
www.litfirepublishing.com
order@litfirepublishing.com

Contents

· · · · · · · · · · · · · · · · · · · ·

LITERARY TITAN

Congratulations!

I am proud to present you with our Literary Titan Book Award.

Your book deserves extraordinary praise and we are proud to acknowledge your dedication,

writing skill and imagination.

The Gold Award is bestowed on books that we found to be perfect in their delivery of original content, meticulous development of unique characters in an organic and striking setting, innovative plot that supports a fresh theme, and elegant prose that transforms words into beautifully written novels.

Thomas Anderson

Editor In Chief

Literary Titan

Dedication

. . . .

For my mom and my grandparents. I'm eternally grateful for the sacrifices you made on my behalf. I love and miss you dearly.

My wife, thank you for taking this journey with me. Without you, I'd be walking aimlessly through life. My love for you is eternal.

My kids, never stop dreaming, never stop searching, believe that you can and you will. I love you.

My Road to Arms

. . . .

I remember a time when all I could think about was getting out of the town where I was raised, Weslaco, Texas. I was so sick and tired of having to work in the fields, picking crops. It was very tiresome work, and it didn't pay much at all. I would spend my weekends and holidays out in someone else's fields when all my school classmates were out having fun either with their other friends or with their families. Ever since I was a kid, all I could think about was breaking this cycle, which my family considered to be our only way of life. I was headstrong yet seen as a dreamer by my own family for wanting to do something else with my life and not wishing to follow in their footsteps.

My journey through madness began with an unchartered road to bear arms, which I first chose to take in the summer of 1992. I was about to begin my senior year of high school, and I didn't have a clue as to what I was going to do after graduation. I had already been a migrant worker for ten years of my life. I knew that I didn't want to continue picking crops in the fields of Michigan or any other state, for that matter. I had to break the cycle, which my family had been stuck on for the past four generations. I wanted something better for myself, but I was afraid because I didn't know anything else other than picking tomatoes, cucumbers, peppers, onions, and strawberries. I was afraid of getting out of this poor colonia (neighborhood) that had been home to me since the age of five. I had made up my mind that fear or anything else in the world was not going to keep me from leaving that place.

One afternoon that summer, a friend of mine called me to let me know that he was thinking of joining the Marines. He asked if I wanted to accompany him to the recruiting office and see what they had to offer. Up until that moment, that phone call, I had never thought of or considered joining the military. When I agreed to go with him, it was simply one friend agreeing to go somewhere with another. The military had never entered my mind as an option for me to leave my hometown or to do something with my life. I was only going somewhere with a friend as a favor and support, nothing else.

On our way to the recruiting office, my friend was telling me why he had decided to join the Marines. Like me, he too wanted to get out of that town and felt that this was his only chance or way of doing so. I kept on thinking of how strange it was that two guys who were raised in tightly knit families wanted nothing to do with this town and were willing to get away from their families. Nothing else crossed my mind during that fifteen-minute ride. I was so lost in my own thoughts of finding a way out that my friend was basically talking to himself because I was not listening. I went through the motions of nodding my head at the right moments and appearing as though I were acknowledging and understanding every word my friend was saying, but I was not even in the vehicle. I was lost somewhere else, looking for a solution to my own dreams of escaping the migrant way of life.

At the recruiting office, we were shown the typical Marine training video along with other recruiting videos, which promised us the world, a strong manhood, educational benefits, and all the many things that military videos make one believe the hype of all the crazy yet exciting adventures a military life entails. I had never seen or heard so many empty promises and lies in my life, yet we saw and heard them in a span of two hours at the recruiters' office. We both walked out of there with a handful of brochures and ASVAB exam dates along with some letters for our parents to sign because we were still under the age of eighteen. To this day, I don't know what took place inside that office that made me want to enlist. All I can think and say is that I fell for the lies and the hype. My friend was excited and couldn't wait to leave for training while I was still trying to figure out what had just taken place. He drove me home and thanked me for having joined him on the next venture in our lives.

As I got off the pickup truck, my grandfather was outside with my grandmother. My grandfather was watering some plants as my grandmother watched idly, sitting on her rocking chair. She had just been diagnosed with terminal cancer about a month earlier and couldn't do much of anything due to her weak condition. I approached her and kissed her on the cheek. She looked very frail and tired. She asked about the papers that I was holding in my hand, and so I took a deep breath and asked my grandfather to stop what he was doing and join us because I had something important to ask them.

My grandparents had raised me since I was six years old, and all my life I had and continued to address them as *Mom* and *Dad*. Up until the moment in which my grandmother asked about the papers in my hand, I had not realized that I was going to be the bearer of some extremely bad news. Nobody else in the family had ever discussed the possibilities of joining the military. For whatever reason, this topic had never been brought up at all, at least not that I could remember. It was this realization that made me feel like the bearer of bad news. Now, my family did push education hard on me, but nobody ever talked about the possibilities of becoming a doctor, a lawyer, a corporate manager, or a pharmacist. No profession was ever pushed on us other than picking crops. In knowing this, one would probably believe that this was why the military was never mentioned either, but I knew in my heart and soul that it wasn't the case. The military had never been mentioned because it was seen by my family as an extremely bad and dangerous thing, yet I had never realized that until this moment.

I faced my grandparents and handed the brochures to them. My grandmother snatched them from me and gave them a quick glance before dropping them on my grandfather's lap. She looked at me and asked me in a very stern voice what I was thinking of doing with those brochures. I took a deep breath and began to plead my case. I talked to them about me not wanting to continue living my life as a migrant worker. I told them about wanting to go out and see what else the world had to offer. I talked to them about my dreams of being able to live in a better neighborhood, in a bigger and better house. I told them about wanting to leave the town of Weslaco, Texas. I lastly told them about my desire to continue my education after high school and how the military would pay for it all and they wouldn't have to worry about making that expense.

As I continued to plead my case, I saw the expressions on their faces and knew that they weren't accepting anything I was saying. My grandfather had a look of defeat and hopelessness. Here was his grandson whom he had raised as his youngest son, telling him that everything he had ever worked for was not enough. I could see how my words had cut through him. I was ungrateful and didn't deserve anything he had ever done for me. He had always seen me as his son, yet on that day, on that moment, his son was lost and my grandfather ceased to recognize the boy in front of him.

My grandmother looked upset, and this thought was confirmed by her actions. As weak and frail as she was, she mustered up all her strength to stand up off her rocking chair. I quickly went for her arm to help her up, but she snapped at me and told me to leave her alone. Shaking with her pain, her anger, and her determination, she managed to stand up and stood directly in front of me. She told me to look at her and listen as she tossed the Marine brochures back at me. I looked at her frail body as she stood in front of me and said, "I'm not going to tell you what to do, but I will say this: if you want me to die, you go right on ahead and join the Marines!" With that said, she turned away ever so slowly and attempted to walk away. She was too weak though and couldn't take but one step. I grabbed her arm to help, but once again, she snapped at me and told me to leave her alone. My grandfather stood up and helped her into the house.

I remained outside, crying in disbelief with the brochures lying on the ground around me. God himself could not do what this frail old lady had just done. Her words pierced through my heart as she single-handedly placed her impending death on me and my decisions. I remember standing out there for a very long time, looking at our tiny house and looking at the sky, trying to find a solution to what had just taken place. I felt ashamed for having hurt my grandparents. How could I be so thoughtless? I picked up the brochures and walked inside the house. I walked directly toward the trash can and threw away all the brochures and paperwork. Becoming a Marine would never cross my mind again.

A month later, I started my senior year of high school and the whole journey of still trying to figure out what to do with my life. By this time, my friend had already taken the military entrance exam known as the ASVAB. He had scored high enough on the exam to where he could get a job in the Marines that he could also use after his military service was completed. When he tried to explain it to me, I didn't quite understand it because he was using the same military jargon that the recruiter had used on him. To be honest, I don't think he understood it at that time either. Fourteen years later, I found out that he had been trained to be a helicopter and airplane engine mechanic.

My grandmother had gotten worse, and my grandfather couldn't work as much out on the fields. I only had to attend school for half a day, so I began working two jobs after school. I worked as a waiter for a Chinese restaurant from 1:00 PM to 10:00 PM and then as a cashier at a local beer store from 10:30 PM to 2:00 AM. I maintained this routine in order to help out with the bills and expenses at home while keeping myself out of the fields at the same time. I still had homework and studying to worry about, so I had to find a way to use every five- or ten-minute break to take care of those things. I would finish my schoolwork at the restaurant between serving tables and on my breaks. Most of my studying and research was then taken care of at the beer store. The schedule was tough on me, but I chose to ignore its toughness and saw it as a means to an end. The cycle of being a migrant worker was going to end with me. What I failed to realize at that time was that my hectic schedule didn't leave me with any time for myself. I was blinded by my own determination and didn't leave room for searching other options or to pursue a goal that could take me beyond graduation. I had no time to rest and even less time to think about my future.

December 5, 1992. It had been cold all week long, yet a very light drizzle made that day even colder and unbearable. We had a nice bonfire going on outside our house to warm one another up as we all talked about times passed. The whole family was there. My mother had been with us for about three days already. One of my uncles had brought her over from Mexico to be able to spend some time with my grandmother. Looking back, I guess it's safe to say that we all felt and knew that the inevitable was approaching. Some of us were just having a tougher time accepting it.

It was about 8:00 PM, and everyone was outside the house except for three people. My eldest brother and I were inside the house, sitting next to my grandmother's bed. She had been a tough woman her entire life. She had picked crops and tended to her husband, her children, and her house throughout her entire adult life. My brother and I held her hand as she looked at us one last time, shed a tear, and passed away. My brother and I sobbed quietly at her side, and shortly after, I heard footsteps running into the house and people crying all around us. Hours later, a family member explained how the flames of the bonfire had risen high above everyone and then the fire had just died out in an instant as if someone had poured water all over it. He said that everyone outside had seen it happen and that they all somehow knew that she had passed away at that exact moment in which the flames had ceased to light up the night.

After her death, many things changed within me. I was mad at her and at God. I had kept my word to her and didn't sign up to join the Marines. Why did she not keep her word to me? Why did she leave me when I desperately needed guidance to find out what to do with my life? I knew then just as I know now that we all must die at one point or another, but I just couldn't understand why it had to happen at that point in my life and in the manner in which it happened. I continued to go through the motions of my senior year at school. The thoughts of not being able to continue my education after graduating continued to run through my mind on a daily basis, yet it didn't seem to bother me as much as it had in the past. My search for something better ended, and now I just wanted to get away.

I graduated from Weslaco High School on May 29, 1993. I was in the top 10 percent of my class, and we were a class of roughly 648 students. A month later, I was on a plane toward Fort Knox, Kentucky; I had enlisted in the army . I kept telling myself that I still kept my word to my grandmother because I never enlisted in the Marines. I kept telling myself that I would be all right and that everything would turn out great. I was scared out of my mind and didn't know what to expect. Little did I know that I had just taken my first step onto what would become a great yet extremely tough journey.

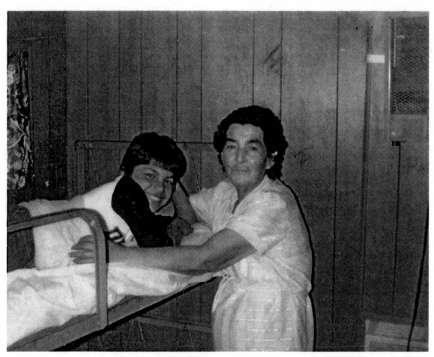

My grandmother and I at a Migrant rest area in Hope,
Arkansas, on our way to Michigan one summer.

Beginnings

. . . .

Since the age of seven, I've been using the power of daydreams and music to escape the situations I don't find favorable to my personal being. They say a kid's childhood is when the imagination runs free without the normal day-to-day barriers of life. Barriers such as work, worrying about bills, wondering about what tomorrow will bring, or even caring for where your next meal is going to come from. These are all matters that seem to be taken for granted nowadays. Kids now worry about the next game that is coming out or is already out and they don't have yet. My own kids worry about frivolous things such as what they're getting for a good grade in school, what we're buying for them at the store, or what new electronic gadget we will be purchasing for them.

Please don't think that I'm complaining about what kids worry about today; my wife and I work hard so that our kids can have and enjoy all the things we could only dream about during our childhood. It just seems hard to adjust to the changes in mentality or mind-set sometimes. This is especially true when we get to sit at home and actually take in everything that our kids have and all the things we have accomplished ourselves.

From the ages of seven to sixteen, my daydreams would take me to faraway places where I could run freely without having to break my back every day for what I believed at that time to be a mediocre life. See, I began picking crops with my grandparents when I was seven years old. My mother lived in Reynosa, Mexico, and I was fortunate enough to have been born in the United States. I guess that even as I lay there inside my mother's womb, I knew which country was the greatest in the world. My mother happened to be visiting her parents in a South Texas border town called San Juan, Texas, when a higher power decided it was time I come out and join the masses living in this great country. I was born in Pharr, Texas, on November of 1974, an American citizen.

I have never met or been given any information regarding my biological father. I don't care to know the reasons behind him not being present or available when I was born. I never have. When I turned fifteen, my mother asked me to sit down in the living room of her small two-bedroom apartment, which she owned in Reynosa, Mexico. I did as asked, wondering what this was all about. My mother began her speech by letting me know that it was time I knew more about my biological father. I quickly stood up, looked her straight in the eyes, and said I never wanted to know anything about that person. I had survived fifteen years of not knowing and making a father figure out of my grandfather; I could continue going through life the same way. Nothing needed to change.

My mother took my statement hard at first and was probably confused as to why I didn't care to learn anything about this person. To be honest, I don't have a concrete answer myself. I don't recall ever wondering who my father was, and if I ever did, I probably blacked it out of my memory. I had spent my childhood looking at other men for guidance and support, mainly, my grandfather. I can say that I hadn't found someone I wanted to emulate once I got older. How could I? Although I was surrounded by great men in my family, I had already learned about hard work, a lesson I began to learn since I was seven. Learning something about this stranger now was not going to change any life lesson I had already been through. In any case, that was the end of our discussion, and it has never been brought up again. Maybe I should have reacted differently and agreed to learn something about the man responsible for my coming into the world.

So what does this have to do with me picking crops at age seven? Well, after I was born, I was living with my mother in Mexico until it was time for me to begin school. My grandparents, along with my mother, made the wise decision of allowing me to obtain an American education, and so I would begin living with my grandparents while my mother continued to live in Mexico. I'm sure this was tough at first. I just can't seem to recall any memories of how difficult this was for my mother and me at such a young age. I do, however, vaguely remember how at age six I was playing outside my grandparents' house and saw them arrive in an old Ford pickup truck pulling a worn-down trailer full of personal belongings. I collapsed and began crying at the sight of their arrival. They had been gone all summer long, and I had missed them so. I had been left behind to spend the summer with their eldest son and his wife while they had migrated north to the state of Michigan in order to work in the fields. Even from such a young age, I was completely overwhelmed by my own emotions that my body could only collapse in reaction to such strong feelings. I didn't know it then, but it would turn out that my body would continue to react like this every time I was overwhelmed with emotions.

This was by all accounts a joyous moment in my life. My grandparents, whom I loved very much, had returned to me, yet I couldn't even muster the strength to run over to them and hug them tightly. It took me a few moments to finally recover my bearings and the assistance of my aunt to finally be able to react as any child would in such a moment. I ran down the porch steps of their house and squeezed my grandfather's leg tightly before he picked me up and hugged me. My grandmother ran around the truck, frantic to know why I was crying and if something bad had happened after witnessing my collapse on their porch. I didn't have an answer as to why I had collapsed; I didn't understand it myself. My aunt was at a loss for answers as well since there really was no reason for me to have reacted the way I did in such a happy occasion. I knew I was happy to see them again, yet it also felt painful.

I remember holding them tightly, crying my eyes out, and asking, begging them to never leave me behind again. To tell me, promise me, that I would be taken wherever they went. I didn't know it at that time, but it turns out I was actually asking to lose my childhood. I was asking to join them in the fields, picking crops for a living at such a young age. In the end, it wasn't so much that my grandparents granted my wishes. Where would I stay? My mother worked long hours at a Zenith fabrication plant, making televisions in Reynosa, Mexico. I'm guessing there was nobody they could trust to babysit me while she worked, at least throughout the summer while my grandparents migrated north. The only recourse they saw fit was to take me with them. So it was; the following summer, at age seven, I became a migrant worker.

We lived in a small wooden house that was about seven hundred square feet in size. That's just a little bit bigger than a regular two-car garage of today's home standards. The house contained three doors: the front door, back door, and the door to our restroom. The middle of the house contained one wall that would separate the house in two basic sections.

The larger section contained my grandparents' bed, common area or living room space, and the kitchen and dining table. Our common area or living room was a small area that measured no more than eight by ten feet.

The smaller section of the house contained two beds and the restroom. There was only one small closet in the entire house. This closet was used by everyone, and it was located inside the restroom. The closets in each of my kids' rooms now are probably three times the size of the closet we had for the entire family back then.

We had a total of three beds in full-the house, two full-size beds and one twin-size bed. This was for a total of six people. My grandparents slept in one; their bed was located immediately upon entering the house in what was also considered our living room area or common area. My two brothers (uncles and my grandparents' youngest boys) slept on the other full-size bed, which was located on the other half of the small house. The twin-size bed was for my sister (aunt and my grandparents' youngest daughter). These beds were placed together and perpendicular to each other.

I did not have a bed. I slept on the floor in front of my grandparents' bed in the common area of the house. I slept on that floor for ten years and didn't get a spot on the beds until my brothers got married and left home to start their own lives.

The first couple of years living there, we had an outhouse for our restroom in the back corner of our small yard. Every time the hole would fill up, we would have to move the outhouse to a different spot of the back yard and cover the old hole up. That backyard had plenty of manure fertilizer. It took us about four years to finally get an actual toilet with running water.

Not having running water for the first couple of years meant we also had to use five-gallon paint cans for our water buckets to shower with. Taking a shower during the winter months of South Texas would take time because we had to first heat up the water on our gas stove and then mix it with cold water inside the five-gallon buckets to an agreeable temperature.

So now every summer, from early May to early October, I would migrate up to Blissfield and Deerfield, Michigan, to work in the fields. We would pick cucumbers, tomatoes, strawberries, cantaloupe, and long banana peppers. Granted, as a seven-year-old kid, there wasn't much I could do with regard to working hard, but a helping hand was a helping hand.

I remember we would be woken up by my grandmother between four thirty and five o'clock every morning so we could all get ready for work and have breakfast before heading out. These are actually some very fond memories I have of my childhood. Smelling the freshly cooked flour tortillas every morning. I was somewhat spoiled because I was such a skinny boy, and everyone believed that I had tapeworms or something of the sorts because I would never gain any weight. My grandmother would make me eat about three warm tortillas with butter, and then I would have breakfast with everyone else in the family. I was growing up alongside my uncles and aunt as though they were my brothers and sister. We were all one family.

Whenever we were clearing crop fields of weeds, we would start work with the daylight. As soon as we could see, we were working. We wouldn't stop working until my grandfather said it was time to go home. We would take a break to eat lunch around noon every day. Our lunch meals were always a fun time for us all because we could relax and joke about anything and everything. My grandfather would actually leave us alone and just enjoy the short time we had away from work. Of course, we were still at the same field. We would open up the tailgate of my grandfather's pickup truck and eat on it and around the truck itself. As long as we had some shade cover around us, we were good to go. We would all give one another a bit of trash-talking depending on where we were all with our individual row or rows of work.

Weeding crops was the easiest of all our jobs. We could walk together with our hoe in hand, taking the weeds out and either telling stories or singing songs that we all knew. Well, at least songs we all thought we knew. There would always be one of us messing up the song, and of course there would be laughter and trash-talking. Sometimes my grandfather would join in on the storytelling. He would tell us of older times of when he was a kid himself.

There were other times when he was worried about something going on back in Mexico with his three daughters and their families. During those times, he would either speed up and work ahead of us or slow down and work behind us. My guess is that he just needed time to collect his thoughts and figure out a solution to whatever was taking place. Keep in mind though that whether he sped up or slowed down to be away from us, there were repercussions to either course of action.

Whenever he sped up and worked ahead of us, we couldn't be caught laughing too much or trying to enjoy ourselves too much with the storytelling and singing because there was work to be done and we were slowing progress down. Depending on how serious he was worried about other matters or whatever was going on in his mind, we would be scolded and told to quit playing around and get to work.

The worst was whenever he would slow down and stay behind us. Then he would find deficiencies in our work, possibly find that we didn't take a weed completely out of the ground or that we missed one somewhere. If this was the case, he would normally yell or grab a piece of hard dirt and throw it at us to grab our attention and let us know how bad we were working. Of course our work was then determined to be bad or of poor service because we were joking, storytelling, or singing away when we were supposed to be focused on our job of weeding out the crops.

There was always something that my grandfather did that bothered all of us. When working in fields, the rows are long, and thus, all our unnecessary equipment remained in the truck so that we wouldn't be lugging it around with us causing us to slow down. Well, it never failed that, on days when it was going to rain, we would be on the far side of the field, either working our way away from the truck or barely working our way back toward it. All of us would look up at the sky and its clouds threatening us with rain. If it rained, we would need to stop weeding and call it a day because otherwise the weeds would stick back to the dirt again and defeat the purpose.

This would cause the farmers to pay us for no reason at all. Once we could guess or determine that rain was about to come down on us, we would all begin to argue among ourselves to figure out who was going to tell my grandfather that rain was coming and that we should stop working and make our way back to the truck. Our intention was twofold: one, to stop working, of course, and two, to make our way toward the truck before the rain came down on us and got us all wet.

Well, once it was decided who was going to approach my grandfather with the statement that we should stop working and head back toward the truck to beat the rain, the person would have to build the courage to do so. Of course, the rest of us would pretend to be working hard while the poor soul approached my grandfather with the request. Thinking back, this was hilarious yet nerve-racking at the same time. See, we all knew what my grandfather's reaction would be, yet we still mustered the courage to try. Either one of my brothers (uncles), my sister (aunt), or I would approach my grandfather (Dad) to let him know that the rain was about to come down on us.

Dad would look up at the sky and then look at us and ask us in a stern voice, "Está lloviendo? Se estan mojando?" Is it raining? Are you getting wet?

The answer would always be "No, pero ya viene el agua, Papa." No, but the rain is coming, Dad.

He would look at us with a disapproving and disappointed look and say, "Sigan trabajando hasta que nos caiga el agua." Continue to work until the rain falls upon us.

And we would. Within minutes we would smell the rain approaching and actually see the wall of rain making its way toward us while we were at least three hundred yards away from our truck or any cover that could shelter us from the rain. Once we began getting wet, Dad would yell at all of us to stop working and run toward the truck so that we wouldn't get wet. I can still picture us all running in the rain toward the truck, laughing at the ridiculousness of it all and knowing that nothing would change the next time that rain would threaten our work.

Picking crops was an entirely different story. We would stay in the fields, working rain or shine. The crop had to be picked no matter what. We would have our gloves on, long-sleeved shirts to protect our arms from all the scrapes and cuts one tends to get from picking crops such as cucumbers, oranges, or grapefruit and to protect us somewhat from the sun.

Once the rain would start coming down, we would all pull out large trash bags and cut holes on the bottom and its sides for our head and arms to go through. They were the best Glad brand raincoats a migrant could have. Not heavy at all to slow us down and good enough to protect our torso from the rain while allowing us free range of motion for the work that had to be done. I'd like to see that as a commercial someday. I bet Glad would get more sales from migrant workers or maybe get a huge lawsuit from the commercial with today's society, which is hell-bent on being politically correct.

I missed my mother something terrible during those initial years of migrating up north. It would be the longest time I'd spend without seeing her on weekends. At least whenever we were back in Weslaco, Texas, a small border town found in the southern tip of Texas, I would see her on weekends and during holidays. This was, of course, if we weren't working.

By now, I had already began calling my grandfather Dad and my grandmother Mom. I think this hurt my mother some, but there was nothing one could do. I was being raised by my grandparents alongside my uncles, aunt, and now a female cousin who was in the same situation that I was. Having been born in the United States, she needed a good education as well. Of course, she also became another helping hand in the fields.

Being that we were a migrant family, it meant that our family's financial income was just above the poverty level. This meant we were a family that benefited from the various government welfare programs that were available to families such as mine. Programs such as food stamps, monthly milk, rice, and cheese rations were just some of the few forms of government assistance that we benefited from.

While in school, we were also given shoes and clothing whenever we needed them. Sadly, these clothing programs were all too familiar to kids who did not need them and whose families were better off than we were. This created an issue with fights in school.

There wasn't a day in school that I didn't have to defend myself from other kids calling me names such as "food stamp kid," "secondhand shoes boy," and "cherry picker." They would make fun of the fact that I would wear the same pants twice or three times a week. Little did they know that it wasn't by choice; I had to wear the same clothes two or three times a week.

I would come home from school and immediately have to change into even more ragged clothing because my "good" pants and shirts would have to be hung up for another day in the week. We had school clothes and play or work clothes. Although these "privileged" kids had plenty to talk about and criticize, I was not about to let them call me names on a daily basis, no, sir. I was a quiet kid, until they pushed the wrong buttons; then, it was hell to pay.

Needless to say, not my grandparents, my mother, or anyone else in the family truly knew what I was going through. Well, at least not to the extent that I was experiencing these situations. While I was in the fifth grade, a counselor must have seen some potential in me and had me take an aptitude exam. I must have scored fairly high on the exam because the following year I was placed in advanced courses, which at that time were called Gifted and Talented. This is where the troubles in school began.

Here was a poor migrant worker seated in an advanced curriculum with kids who had never had to work during their childhood. I was the oddball, the poor, uneducated kid who didn't belong, and they never hid their thoughts or feelings about me. My grandparents were being called in every week because of all the fights I was involved in. For the most part, my family was always in shock, or so they acted as they were because I was such a scrawny kid. It used to be said that a broomstick had more curves than I did.

So when my family was being told that I was constantly fighting against other kids, it was somewhat difficult for them to believe that someone as skinny as I was could actually be involved in so many fights and actually be winning them. It got so bad that my grandmother finally signed a consent form at the principal's office, allowing the school to spank me with a wooden paddle anytime I ended up in the office for disciplinary issues.

After a few spankings with that paddle, the fighting stopped.

Since I wasn't fighting anymore, there had to be something else I could do to make all those white kids and coconuts (Mexicans thinking they're white) shut up and leave me alone. One night while doing my homework, I simply decided to be as good as they were in class and show them that I did belong in the advanced curriculum.

Don't think that I was always a fighter. I actually didn't become a fighter until my mother and my aunt forced me to defend myself against other kids in Reynosa, Mexico.

Up until I was seven years old, I was pretty much a pushover. Other kids my age would make fun of me or belittle me because I was quiet and never outspoken. I would go into the house all dirty, not from playing but from being beaten up by other kids outside.

My mother, being a strong single mom, wouldn't try to comfort me, much less shelter me from the beatings I was getting. Instead, she would always ask me why I didn't defend myself or fight back. I truly never had an answer other than I was afraid of the other kids. They seemed meaner and much stronger than I was. It turns out they were just regular bullies who lived nearby.

I remember one particular afternoon. I was outside playing with one other kid named Mario, and we were both seven years old. We were just kicking a soccer ball around, having a good time, or so I thought. Before I knew it, two other kids showed up. One of them was my age, and the other one was about two years older; they were brothers.

The kid who was my age was named Javier, but everyone just called him Javi. His brother was Sebastian, and he had a bad reputation amongst all the other kids to constantly be causing trouble for everyone and beating up anyone he didn't care for. I'm guessing that day was my day to be the target.

In any case, Javi and Sebastian both began to kick the soccer ball around with Mario and me. At first, everything seemed fine, but then the name-calling began. Javi began calling me every name in the book, and I just continued playing trying to ignore the name-calling. Soon enough, Sebastian chimed in and then egged Mario to join in as well. I couldn't understand what had just happened. Mario had been playing with me for a while, and now he joined in on the name-calling with those two punks.

As with all forms of bullying, the actions of kids begin to escalate when given a little bit of time. This case was no different. Soon the name-calling moved on to pushing and shoving me around. The pushing around led to Sebastian kicking the ball as hard as he could toward my face. I was lucky a couple of times and was able to dodge the ball hitting me, but then Javi and Mario got a cue from the oldest, and they held me in place so that the ball would hit me.

After a few hits with the ball, I was already crying, and the other two let go of me as I collapsed onto the dirt beneath me.

As I was down on the ground, I felt a kick on the back of my legs. My crying must have been loud enough for my mother and aunt to hear because they had already made their way out to the balcony of the second-floor apartment and were watching intently as I was getting the crap beaten out of me. None of us kids had realized my mother and aunt were up there watching. Through the sounds of my own crying and the name-calling of the other three kids, I was able to hear my mother's strong voice.

"Sergio, es mejor que te levantes y te defiendas por que si no lo haces, te va ir peor conmigo despues de que terminen ellos contigo!" Sergio, it's best you get up and defend yourself from these kids because if you don't, I'm going to whoop you worse after those kids are done with you!"

I remember listening in disbelief. How could she be threatening to beat me some more after these kids were done with me? My own mother. I looked up toward her and saw that she meant business as she continued to yell at me to get up and fight.

Listening to her, seeing that intense look in her eyes, along with a mixture of my own fear, pain, and anger, must have done something within me. I don't know what exactly. I just know that I was able to get up and began fighting in a mad rage.

It was as if I was blinded by my own fury as I punched and kicked my way through all three kids. Even after all three kids were beaten down to the ground, I kept on kicking them shouting at them yet still crying in an uncontrollable rage. I hated it that it had come to this, and I wanted them to pay for it, for pushing me to this point. Overwhelmed with my own emotions, my body was shaking uncontrollably.

It wasn't until I heard my mother's voice again that I began to calm down. This time, though, her voice was different. She was sweet again, telling me that everything was okay; I had defended myself and did what needed to be done. She had made her way downstairs toward me. I felt her hands around me as she held me tight and hugged me there in the midst of all the chaos that had just taken place. She grabbed my hand and walked me back into the house as the other kids somehow picked themselves up and walked away crying and hurting just as much as I had been.

Mom and I inside my grandparents' house in
Weslaco, Texas, during Christmas.

Me, picking cucumbers when I was ten years old in Blissfield, Michigan.

Camp where we would get housed every summer that we worked in Blissfield, Michigan. Second door from the left was my family's room. Nine of us stayed in that room at one time. The small, darker building on the left side of the picture was used for our showers and restrooms.

Learning English

· · · · · · · · · · · · · · · · · · · ·

Being a young migrant worker in the state of Michigan was not an easy thing. Child labor laws were already in effect, and the fields would be checked periodically by the city officials to ensure that no children were being used in the fields. Yet somehow, the farmers in the area where we worked all seemed to know when their fields were going to receive a surprise visit, because we would be told to get off the field and go sit in the pickup trucks or vans of all our parents.

It was always interesting to see and try to interact with the city officials or inspectors. I say this because, although they would always find us sitting inside the bed of the pickup trucks, they would also see that our clothes and shoes were just as dirty as those of adults who were working the fields.

Our English wasn't good at all the first couple of years, and so answering the officials' questions was always an interesting challenge. Looking back, I can laugh at those moments as I recall the officials literally yelling at us in English as though the louder they got, the more we would understand.

As the years went by and I could understand their questioning, I remember them asking us why we were so dirty. We would simply respond by saying that we were outside the vehicles, playing. Of course, the officials would still be perplexed at our response and still ask us again how we got so dirty by just playing.

I remember poking at one of the officials to grab his attention and then hand-signaling at the entire field that surrounded us, trying to show them, "Look at where we are, we are surrounded by dirt." I don't think the officials realized that there were no grassy playgrounds in the fields where we worked. Their facial expressions were always hilarious to watch, and we would spend hours mocking them afterward. Fun times.

Another harsh fact, at least for me, is that we were mandated to attend summer school at least three times a week in order to appease to the city inspectors. The problem with attending summer school is that I was constantly getting into fights with all the white kids who were in class with me.

It sucked being a migrant kid in a predominantly white school, especially when all or most of those kids had a far better life than I had or at least a more privileged life. Every Monday morning would begin the same way; the classroom teacher would ask everyone how our weekend was and what we did during our days off from school.

Every kid would then chime in and comment on how they went fishing, to the zoo, to the park, and some would even mention camping. I, on the other hand, spent the weekend working, picking crops.

Talk about being aggravated over such a simple question about what I had done during the weekend.

There were times when I would just remain quiet and not partake in the class discussion, but of course, some teachers had to probe and ask in a loud voice as though to make me understand their questions of what I had done.

The other kids already knew what I had done; it was very common for the Mexican kids to be the workers on some of their fathers' farms.

My decision to remain quiet and not respond would normally end up with the other kids giggling and laughing since they knew perfectly well what I had done. It was not a good feeling to sit there week after week, knowing that I didn't have a good story to tell like the rest of the kids did. Every time this occurred, I would hold my anger in until it was time for recess.

Come recess, those kids were mine, and not a person in the world could ever stop me from giving them the whooping of a lifetime. Thus, every week, the farmer we worked for would receive a phone call from the school with the notification that I and other kids from our working camp had fought and beat other kids during recess.

We would be sent home, and one of the parents from the camp would have to stop working to go pick us up and take us to the field. So not only were we causing problems at school with our fighting, but we were also causing our families to lose money by having to spend time away from work to pick us up. Talk about being in trouble.

The same would happen all the time; we would get to our respective parents in the fields and have to answer their questions as to why we were fighting.

Our answer was always the same, "The gringos were laughing at us because we work in the fields! They laugh at us every week because of our clothes and the way we look."

There were even times when I would end up getting myself into more trouble by being stupidly brave and telling my grandparents, "If you don't want me to fight the gringos, then don't send me to the stupid school!"

This burst of frustration and anger never ended well for me. It would always end up with my grandfather grabbing a cucumber or whatever vegetable or fruit we were picking at that time and just throwing it at me. I don't think he ever missed, and for some stupid reason, I never felt it coming my way or prepared for it even though it had already happened hundreds of times. I would always get struck on my legs or on my back, with a stern look and command for me to shut up and get to work. These were not fun times.

My attitude toward school would soon change. My grandfather decided to show me the importance of school by forcing me to learn the English language in a fast and stern manner. Not long after expressing my disinterest in school, I was told by my grandfather that every evening after work I was to sit with him in front of the television and watch the news.

We only had the basic television channels on our television, and being that we were in Michigan, all the local channels were English-speaking channels only. My grandparents didn't know any English, and they relied entirely on me and the rest of their children to interpret for them.

At age seven, I knew very little English and not nearly enough to interpret what was being said on the news. Yet I was expected to interpret everything as though I were an English professor. So I did what any other kid my age and in my position would do in order to survive this ordeal. I would watch the television screen and come up with my own stories to tell my grandfather. The stories would, of course, depend entirely on the images on the screen. With the regular news, this tactic actually worked and kept me out of trouble.

The weather was a different story though.

I was too young to understand the importance of the weather, but I learned its significance very quickly. The weather is an important factor for migrant workers trying to make a living.

How was I supposed to know this at such a young age?

Well, it only took a few wrong guesses about the weather for me to realize its importance. At least the importance of me surviving the following day without a scolding or spanking with a thick leather belt. Have you ever seen Mexican leather belts? They are thick and heavy.

I now believe my grandfather knew I was just making up stories when it came to the regular news. How else could one explain how a seven-year-old could interpret the fast-paced material with such ease when he was barely learning English?

It was all a test of sorts to see if I would catch on to the importance of actually paying attention and learning in school. I still remember how my grandfather would reposition himself on his chair just before the weather segment would begin. I'm quite certain that he could decipher the weather images far better than I could, yet I was held responsible for the correct interpretation.

The weather segment would begin, and I would just stare blindly at the television screen, trying to make sense of what was being said and the various different-colored arrows on the map. These were very stressful moments, yet I always figured I had a 50 percent chance of getting it right. This thought gave me some comfort, but not much because I knew the wrong interpretation would be disastrously clear the following day while we were out on the fields, trying to earn some money. My older siblings (uncles and aunt) would all leave and walk out of our little camp apartment because they already knew that the news could lead to some serious repercussions. I had no backup.

I would go ahead and come up with my best prediction of the next day's weather so that my grandfather would know what to prepare for in the fields. I would always go to bed that evening hoping and praying that my storytelling would pan out to be correct the next day.

How many rainy clouds were placed on the map so that I could predict light rain or thunderstorms?

Would we need to load raincoats onto the truck, or would we be okay with our trusty Glad trash bags if light rain was being predicted? I remember waking up every morning and immediately being nervous. I would walk outside and look up at the sky, trying to will it toward my predictions. How clear or cloudy was it? Should I expect to feel the heavy leather belt later on that day?

This was no way to start the day, not for a seven-year-old. I would just stand outside, looking up, and then my grandfather would follow suit and look at the sky with me. Not only would he make his own observations of the current weather, but he would also even ask me to repeat my weather interpretations from the previous evening news. The pressure and stress would keep me on pins and needles the entire day.

I think the days when I was quickly proven wrong in the early morning hours were the best for me. I say this because this meant that I didn't have to be worried all day about my news forecast being right or wrong. I just had to prepare myself for a scolding or a spanking or both. It was always easier for me to prepare myself mentally for the punishment than to spend all day worried about whether or not I had given the correct weather forecast.

Needless to say, this daily ritual cemented the mind-set of the importance of school, and I quit complaining about it very quickly.

On one occasion, my grandparents took me on a drive through the town of Blissfield, Michigan. I was worried because nobody else from the family went with us. I kept looking at my grandmother and then at my grandfather as he drove through town until my nerves forced me to inquire about the reason for this particular trip. My grandmother explained that we needed a "new" truck or van, and we were driving around looking at houses to see if we would find a truck or van that was for sale.

I got excited right away; I was being taken on a special trip, just me, alone. I stretched my neck as much as I could to help in the search for our new family vehicle. After a few turns through some of the neighborhoods, my grandfather spotted a van with a For Sale sign on the windshield. He stopped in front of the house, and we all got off the truck in a hurry to go take a closer look at the van. I didn't know what we were looking for exactly, but I remember enjoying myself as I walked around the van with my grandparents, listening to them comment on the wheels, the body, and wonder about the price since there wasn't one listed on sale sign.

After a few minutes, an older gentleman stepped out of the house to greet us. He was a kind-looking man and looked older than my grandfather. He shook my grandfather's hand, said hello to my grandmother, and then patted the top of my head as he began to ask if we were interested in the van. My grandfather asked me right away what the older gentleman had said. I understood immediately what my role in this trip was—I was the interpreter.

My grandfather told me right away to ask the man for the price on the van. I collected my thoughts momentarily as I turned to face the older man and ask in a very broken English, "How much?"

The older man smiled at me and answered, "$1,200."

I once again paused momentarily to gather my thoughts and go over the number in my mind to ensure I got the translation correct. I turned toward my grandparents and let them know that the older man had said $1,200.

My grandfather looked at me, upset with the number I just gave him, and smacked me on the back of my head. "Eso no puede ser. Preguntale otra vez el precio." That can't be correct. Ask him again for the price.

I began to rub the back of my head as I slowly went over the translation in my head and asked the older man again, "How much"?

He smiled at me again and, in a louder tone, repeated the same amount, "$1,200."

I looked down at my feet, back up at the man, then slowly turned again toward my grandparents.

"Papa, el señor dice que el precio de la van es $1,200." Dad, he said the price of the van is $1,200.

My grandfather now looked at me with a look of disgust and frustration, turned toward my grandmother, and said, "Este niño me esta contando cuentos otra vez." This boy is telling me stories again.

He turned back toward me and smacked the back of my head even harder this time. "Preguntale otra vez." Ask him again.

I was now on the verge of tears as I rubbed the back of my head and looked at the older man, once again pausing to go over the translation in my mind, and asked a third time, "How much"?

The older man looked at me bewildered, wondering why my grandfather was smacking me, and then looked at my grandfather and told him in a loud, stern voice, "One thousand two hundred dollars, sir," and shrugged his shoulders, as if asking why I was being smacked around.

Now matters heated up even more for my grandfather. Why was this old white man raising his voice at my grandfather? More importantly, what the hell did I say to the old man that caused this whole situation?

My grandfather began to scold me about my incorrect translation and continued to get more upset as the words became louder and his hand gestures became more threatening.

The older man must have seen what was about to happen next and so decided to intervene by tapping on my grandfather's shoulder and holding his palms open, telling him to calm down and relax, trying to deescalate the situation. He then looked at me and said, "Hold on, wait a minute," and rushed into his house. As we waited outside, my grandfather was now puzzled, wondering what the heck just took place, and we all wondered whether or not the old man was going to come back out or not.

A few moments passed, and we saw the door swing open as the old man came back out with a piece of paper in his hand. He handed the piece of paper over to my grandfather so he could see what was written on it. My grandfather looked at the writing on the paper, and his face lit up immediately with a big, old grin as he showed my grandmother what was written down.

Meanwhile, I was still left wondering what was taking place and what made my grandfather so happy all of a sudden. My grandfather looked at me and began to laugh as he began to rub the back of my head playfully and told me that the old man was selling the van for $1,200.

I let out a sigh of relief while in my head I was saying, *Dad, that's what I've been telling you this whole time.*

As the years passed, English became easier for me. I was able to read, write, and translate, but I was still having problems speaking it properly or without a heavy accent. The reason for this, I think, is that living in the southernmost part of Texas, an area known as the Rio Grande Valley, does not necessarily call for the effective speaking of the English language.

This entire area is a set of small border towns situated right on the Rio Grande River, which divides our country from Mexico. About 90 percent of the population is of Mexican descent, and every business you go to will speak to you in Spanish rather than English. The sad thing is that, even if you continue speaking to people in English, they continue to speak back to you in Spanish.

This can become truly frustrating for people who don't speak Spanish. My wife, for example, is Albanian, and although she understands some Spanish, she is not able to speak it or able to hold a conversation in Spanish. She has to tell everyone that she doesn't speak Spanish and that she doesn't understand it. What's funny and infuriating all at once is that some people actually get mad and ask her why she doesn't speak any Spanish.

To that, I always laugh and respond, "This is the United States of America, isn't it?"

I always tell my wife to get back at those people and begin speaking Albanian to them and see how they react or respond. Needless to say, she has never heeded my advice; but man, would I love to see that situation unfold.

While in school, I never really needed to speak English unless I had a class presentation or if I had questions for the teachers. Even then, most teachers would also speak Spanish to us, and thus, our English speaking was not practiced on a daily basis. Going home after school, I would revert to speaking Spanish entirely because neither my grandparents nor my mother spoke any English. Spanish was and continues to be the family's spoken language.

It wasn't until after I joined the United States Army that I actually began to improve my English-speaking abilities. This was mostly because my chain of command could barely understand what I was saying.

I tell my wife and those individuals close to me that I used to sound like Al Pacino's character Tony Montana in the movie *Scarface* . My accent was horrible, and I had a tough time getting my statements across to my fellow soldiers and the sergeants who were in charge of me.

Now, every time I hear someone with a heavy accent, I remember the tough times I used to have when people could not understand what I was saying, and I can only imagine the strain that I would put them through in trying to decipher the words that were coming out of my mouth.

It didn't take long after I arrived at my first duty station, Fort Hood, Texas, that I was told by my squad leader, Sergeant Bess, that I needed to figure out a way to improve my English speaking because nobody could understand me. He also told me that, if need be, I would be sent to an English as a Second Language (ESL) class and that it would reflect negatively on my military record. That was all I needed to hear.

That same evening, I called my mother over the phone and told her I was not going to be calling her as often anymore so that I could work on my English-speaking skills. I also quit hanging around other Hispanic soldiers and only hung out with white guys and black guys for about a year.

I did this so that I could be forced to speak English the entire time and improve my speech. I think my struggles paid off in the end although my wife does still catch me from time to time saying a few words with a pretty heavy accent or with a Hispanic swirl that makes us both laugh at my different speech patterns.

Words such as *skillet* , I end up pronouncing as *skeelet*, and *bully* ends up coming out of my mouth as *booly*.

What can I say? I'm still learning.

Me, working at a sugar beets field while I was
fifteen years old in Blissfield, Michigan.

No More Fields

. . . .

I had been working in the fields as a migrant worker since I was seven years old. Nine years of literally breaking my back before I was even fully developed as a teenager or young adult. Most kids my age couldn't wait to be teenagers, couldn't wait to be able to drive, couldn't wait to be allowed to go out late at night with their friends. Me, I couldn't wait to turn sixteen so that I could actually get a paying job that was not in the fields. I remember thinking that I would work anywhere as long as it got me out of picking fruits and vegetables. I had spent my entire childhood weekends, holidays, and summers picking crops. I just had to break away from that way of life, and I could not wait.

I turned sixteen during my sophomore year of high school. I was already doing what I could in school to not have to work on the weekends anymore. This meant I had to join school clubs that would take me to school competitions during the weekends. Granted, I did not compete every single weekend, but any weekend away from picking crops was a great weekend.

Throughout middle school and high school, I became a member of the computer science club, math club, Business Professionals of America (BPA), and finally, the law enforcement club. I would even tutor other students after school just so that I could stay out of the fields as much as possible. Not being able to participate in any sports because of our early withdrawal at the end of every school year to migrate up north and the late entrance at the beginning of every school year for the same reason left me with limited options.

My grandparents would always pull us out of school at the beginning of May, and we wouldn't begin school until mid or late October every year. Being migrant workers also meant that none of us had any medical insurance should we get hurt or injured in any way. For these reasons, sports were out of the question.

I began applying for jobs the day after my sixteenth birthday. I remember my grandfather was dead set against this idea, and he tried to discourage me from pursuing it by letting me know that he would never drive me to any job that was not in the fields. He was not about to spend gas money on my ridiculous endeavors. This pretty much meant that asking for a car was definitely out of the question as well.

I remember walking over to a neighbor's house and asking them for a ride to a job interview at a local Chinese restaurant, Red Peppers. I had to iron my best school pants and shirt in secret so that my grandparents wouldn't ask me a million questions and try to keep me from the interview.

After I prepared my clothes, I still had to hide the clothes from them and sneak out of the house just to go for a job interview. Who would have thought that looking for a job would make me feel like such a criminal in my own house? So I snuck away from the house, got dressed at my neighbor's house, and went for my interview. It seems funny now, but I actually interviewed for a busboy position at the restaurant.

At the job interview, I was a nervous wreck as I waited to be seen by the owner. I was not nervous about the interview itself. I was fearing for my life because I truly did not know what would happen back home if I was told that I had the job and had to break the news to my grandparents. I was so determined to get a job, but I had not planned or prepared for telling my grandparents.

How would they take the news? Would they actually support my decision and help me with transportation to and from the job? Or would I be punished for having gone against their wishes and be forced to quit? All I could do was expect the worst while at the same time wish for the best with regard to my interview. There was no turning back. I had to push through and figure out a way to make this work out for me. One way or another, I was done with picking crops. Either my family supported my decision or I would fight them all the way until they gave in. The only thing I knew for sure as I sat on a chair, waiting to be interviewed, was that I was not about to give up on my dream to have a "normal" job.

The actual interview didn't take long at all. How many questions can actually be asked when applying for a busboy slot? I thanked the owner for interviewing me and shook his hand as he told me that he would give me a call within the next two days. This news only increased the fear I was already feeling. I remember my neighbor asking me all kinds of questions on the ride home. At least I think he asked a lot of questions; I could hear him speaking, but I couldn't make out any of the words because I could not stop thinking of how to break the news to my grandparents. I had at least two days before I heard anything, and I was already beginning to panic.

Once we arrived at the neighbor's house, I exited the car and thanked him for his help. As I began to walk toward my grandparents' house, the neighbor stopped me and reminded me that I had to change out of the clothes I was wearing. I was so concerned about facing my grandparents that I had forgotten all about having sneaked out of the house in the first place. I rushed into my neighbor's house and changed out of my good clothes. On my way out of the house, the neighbor stopped me again and asked what I was going to do if I got the job. I didn't have an answer. I told him that I had not thought it through that far, and just stood there by the door, frozen. He laughed, patted me on the back, and wished me luck. Turning around and opening that door seemed like an eternity. Knowing an argument was waiting for me at home was a paralyzing thought.

On my walk home, I thought of all the possible lies I could say and ways I could possibly go about starting a job without my grandparents knowing. Sadly, none of my ideas would work. How was I supposed to explain being out of the house past ten on school nights? Who would give me a ride to and from work every evening? What about the weekends and the additional dirty clothes? I had to come clean with my plans to hold a job that didn't involve picking crops. I had to face them. I had to tell them that I was done migrating north. That picking oranges and grapefruit in our town was not for me. That I wanted more out of life.

Doing so without sounding ungrateful for the life they had provided was the tough part. I didn't know it at that moment, but it was a lesson I would never forget. Thinking back, I am not sure if I was afraid of my grandparents or if I feared somehow letting them down for not wanting a life that they had had and provided for all their kids. They had raised me and cared for me as their own son, not as their grandson. They spoiled me when they could with what they could. They had passed on a strong work ethic, which I was now taking in a different direction. It was change, and change can be a fearsome obstacle at times. Maybe they were not as close-minded as I have always thought them to be. Maybe they simply feared the new path that I was taking at such a young age. Yes, they too had worked all their lives since they were kids. Hard work was a part of their lives, my life. It wasn't seen as a choice in life. It was just seen as life. So I walked home with all these thoughts running through my head. I remember literally shaking with fear at what was about to take place. I even questioned my own thinking, my goals, my strong desire to break the cycle that our family was in. Was my life really that bad?

I made it onto our small yard and immediately heard the television on. My grandparents were watching the news as I walked onto the small porch and opened the screen door. I walked inside with my good clothes from the interview on my arm. I paused by the door as my grandparents looked at me and looked at the clothes I was holding.

My grandmother began the questioning by asking me where I was and what was I doing with an extra set of clothes. I slowly walked over to our kitchen area, which was only about twenty feet from the door. I grabbed a chair and placed it in front of them. I could see their puzzled look, not quite knowing what explanation I was about to give. I began by reminding them that the only three people who could work in the fields were my grandfather, my cousin who lived with us, and me. I pointed out how my grandmother was already too frail for the hard labor of picking crops. Even with these facts in place, my grandparents seemed to be standing their ground and not liking the idea of me wanting to give up the field life. It was, after all, the one and only thing our family had ever done to make ends meet.

My grandfather was always the type of man who didn't care for "long" speeches and always preferred to jump onto the matter at hand. He interrupted my rant and pointed at the extra clothes I had been holding. "Y eso? Porque traes esa ropa en la mano? A donde fuiste?" And that? Why are you carrying extra clothes with you? Where did you go?

I took a deep breath, looked at the both of them, and told them I had gone to a job interview at Red Peppers, the Chinese restaurant across the street from the high school's football stadium. I remember having to repeat the statement because they both just stared at me as though I had spoken in English. Then they just looked at each other in shock at what they had just heard. I had gone against the grain in the past as a kid, but this had to have been my boldest step to date.

In an attempt to stabilize the situation, I continued with my rant to keep my grandparents from speaking or even having a moment to react. I explained the particulars of the job, should I get hired. I would be walking to the job from school after my last class. This was helpful since my grandfather did not have to worry about wasting gas money to take me to work. He would only have to pick me up afterward. Unless, of course, he wanted me to walk home in the night after I got done at work. As strict as they were, I knew walking home would not be an option.

My next pitch to them was the fact that I would also be getting tips every night that I worked. I promised them that I would give them my entire check every two weeks and that I would only keep the tips for my own spending. This was my attempt to pay them off on my plans. I told them my studies would not falter in any way. That I would take care of as much of the bills as I could and, if needed, I would get a second job in the summer to help out even more. They were still silent, staring, when I finally made the one statement they must have known was coming. "Yo no quiero seguir trabajando en las labores y no quiero regresar a Michigan." I don't want to continue working in the fields, and I don't want to go back to Michigan.

Surprisingly, they took my statement fairly well. They didn't even argue with me and agreed to give my plan a chance. They both knew we would not be making any money in the fields since only three of us would be able to work and the money earned would not be worth the breaking of our backs. We were no longer a family of seven that could work long hours in the sun to barely be able to make ends meet. Our workforce was cut in half, yet the workload would remain the same, and they knew it.

I was glad to have been able to get through to them, but I was also saddened by the fact that they were seeing my plans as me being ashamed of our background and our work history. To this day, I don't know if my family has ever understood my reasons for wanting something else other than picking crops. I have never felt ashamed for my upbringing. If anything, I've always been proud of the strong work ethic my grandparents instilled in me, and the memory of my childhood continually humbles me when I see the few things I have accomplished in life.

The funny thing about my new job is that nobody in my family had ever eaten Chinese food, not even me. My grandparents, along with their brothers and sisters, had always told us that Chinese food was nothing but rats and dogs. Why I went along with those beliefs is beyond me now, but back then, they were pretty convincing. It's pretty sad to admit this now, but because of these beliefs, it took me almost two months to even try the food being sold at the restaurant. Once

I tried it though, I was hooked. I loved everything about the food. I couldn't get enough of it. I remember taking food to the house and everybody was afraid to even try it. I even called my uncles to come over and give the food a try, but nobody would. Their thoughts and beliefs were embedded too deep that they would not even get near the food.

I remember the restaurant I worked at would have a buffet until 9:00 PM, but we wouldn't close the restaurant until 10:00 PM. I was in charge of ensuring we would only order the needed food for the buffet once it got close to 9:00 PM. I would always ask the cooks to cook more of whatever meal I wanted to take home. This was because we would always throw away whatever food was left over from the buffet, so I had to make sure that what was left over was something I wanted to take home. This was just one of the perks of working there.

Time went by, and my grandfather ended up not minding picking me up from work every day. I like to think that he actually enjoyed listening to my stories from work. The funny way customers demanded certain things or complained about others. Our rides home have always been memorable for me. I don't think we had ever talked as much. I think he was somewhat excited to hear someone talking about a different type of work and not just the fields. It was all new to him, just as it was for me too. One day, though, our conversation veered to the subject of me being able to have my own car. This immediately kicked off an argument between us.

My grandfather did not agree with me at all on this matter. He said I was too young and that we did not have enough money to purchase a car. I explained to him that I was old enough to get a driver's permit and that I had already saved some money to buy a used car. That night, we must have argued the entire way home, and then it continued on afterward with my grandmother. How was I going to get insurance for the car being a minor? Whom would it be registered under? Up until the point when these questions were asked, I had never imagined that my grandparents wouldn't help me with the insurance or the registration.

These obstacles had never crossed my mind. I knew they would fight me on the actual purchase, but never on these other matters. I hadn't prepared for these questions. I didn't know how to respond or how to counter them. I was upset at them, but mostly, I was mad at myself for not thinking of these issues. I was about to begin my senior year of high school in a few months, and I knew that I was going to need a second job to be able to keep up with the house bills and all the school expenses that came with being a senior. I remember going to bed, feeling defeated that night. As I was shocked and upset, it took me a few hours just to fall asleep. I kept going over other possible options or solutions and could not come up with any.

The next day, I woke up determined to figure out a solution to my problem. Worst-case scenario, I would wait until after I started my last year of high school to purchase a car. This way, I could turn eighteen and be able to get the driver's license on my own without the help or consent of my grandparents. I still had the issues of insurance and registration to worry about, though. I told myself that I had a few more months to worry about that and come up with a solution; until then, I could save up more money for a car. This meant that I had to hold off on looking for a second job as well. There was absolutely no way my grandfather would chauffeur me around to two different jobs and back home.

So my senior year of high school began, and everything was going as good as could be expected. I was still in the advanced curriculum, which was awesome, I was voted president for the law enforcement club at school, and I had become a waiter at Red Peppers. The promotion to waiter was very helpful because I was now getting double in tips and working more hours as well. Things surely became far more interesting at work as a waiter. Some of our customers were very peculiar about their drinks and food orders.

I once had a customer order Peking duck, and he wanted it to be spicy. When I brought his food over, he quickly complained that his meal was not spicy enough. The thing about this particular customer was that he didn't just complain about the meal; the guy chose to belittle my skills as a waiter because I had failed to listen to his specific request. I took it all in, apologized, took his meal back to the kitchen, and told the cooks to make it as hot as they could possibly make it; if I recall correctly, I asked the cooks to ensure the damn duck burned the guy's ass to hell. Of course, the cooks happily obliged my request. A few moments later, I returned to the customer with his "fixed" meal. Poor guy couldn't get enough water afterward. I actually took him a pitcher full of water and ice since his mouth was burning up. I'm sure his ass burned later that evening as well.

Some customers were regulars yet "special." I say *special* because it was important to know whom they were with. There were a few men who would show up from time to time with someone else other than their wife. They would show up one day out of the week with their wife and kids if they had any and then show up again on the weekend with their younger, hotter mistress. The only good thing about those men was that, if you caught on to what they were doing and still treated them with professionalism every single time regardless of whom they were with, they left hefty tips.

Wintertime was our busiest time of year. We would always be inundated with folks from the northern part of the country since South Texas was much warmer than their hometowns. They would always come into the restaurant in large groups and always requested separate checks. I must say that this ordeal was pretty stressful when I first became a waiter, but with time, it was actually a cool challenge.

These folks were funny though; most of them would leave little notes or messages on their bills for us to read afterward. The writing on the notes, of course, relied entirely on the service we provided to them. I remember one day an old lady who was part of a large group of about twenty individuals left me a fifty-cent tip. The kicker was on the bill that was left behind. The old lady wrote on the receipt that my tip would have been doubled had I served her some more water. I sure missed out; I could have had an entire dollar if only I had served her some more water.

Working there was a blast. I met some very interesting people and worked with some very cool folks who taught me a lot not only about the importance of professionalism but also about the importance of having fun on the job. Like any other job in the world, it can have its great moments and its difficult ones. It is left to us to make the best of it no matter what. If you are dreading work on your way to it, it just becomes hard labor regardless of how easy it may be.

By the time the holiday season came around, I had saved about six hundred dollars in tips and was ready to look for a used car. I didn't really care for its looks; I needed transportation, so the make and model of the car didn't matter to me. I discussed the matter again with my grandfather, and when he looked at me as though I were swearing at him, I decided to simply hand the money over to him and ask him to please take me to look for a car or, if he chose, to do it by himself. I think it was at that moment that he realized how serious I was about this. The one thing he could fire back at me was that I still wasn't eighteen years old and didn't have a driver's license. I told him I had already scheduled an appointment for my driver's exam on the day after my eighteenth birthday. Once again, I surprised him.

At this point in time, my grandmother's health had gotten critical. She had been fighting cancer for almost a year now, and the fight was not going her way. I pleaded with my grandfather and my grandmother to please support my decision. I wasn't just doing this for me; I informed them how I needed the car to be able to look for a second job because paying for all the bills of the house was becoming tougher to do with just my waiting job. I told them I had a few friends working in other places whom I could probably seek help from and I could get hired at one of their jobs. After having made my closing argument, my grandmother asked my grandfather to go ahead and look for a car that I could purchase and that everything else would surely sort itself out. The whole matter of vehicle registration and insurance would somehow be resolved in time.

About two weeks later, I went straight home from school since I didn't have to work that day. As I walked up the street toward the house, I saw a car parked outside. I figured someone was visiting, and simply continued walking on ahead, not thinking anything of it. I walked into the house, kissed my grandmother on the forehead as she lay on her bed, and hugged my grandfather, who was sitting by her side.

My grandmother was pretty frail by now, yet she seemed very happy for some strange reason. I quickly walked over to the other side of the house and placed my books down, when I heard my grandfather calling for me. I stopped and paused; I hadn't even asked if anyone was visiting or whose car was parked outside. My grandfather called me again. I walked over to the bed and stood there looking at the both of them. "Yes, Dad?" He looked at me, smiling, then said, "Tenemos algo para ti." We have something for you. At that moment, my grandmother began to move ever so slowly underneath her thin blanket and stretched her hand out, grabbed my grandfather's hand, and then they both handed me a set of car keys.

I was in shock. I had left matters in their hands and had stopped asking about the car business altogether. The beautiful smile on my grandmother's frail face and the gleaming look in my grandfather's eyes were very touching yet extremely paralyzing. I was holding a set of car keys in my hand. Keys to my own car. The car that was parked outside that I hadn't even bothered to look over closely as I walked into the house because I figured someone was visiting us. It took a few more seconds for it all to finally sink in and make sense in my mind. I then jumped up, excited at the idea of having my own car. I hugged and kissed them both tightly, thanking them for everything. With my eyes beginning to well with tears, I quickly ran outside to see the car.

The car was a 1971 Dodge Charger, two-tone in color, yellow over black. It was a bumblebee with air shocks that could be aired up from the rear bumper. Back then as now, I have never known much about cars, nor have I ever cared to learn. I am not mechanically inclined in any way, shape, or form.

The seats of the car were completely torn, and there was a wide, gaping hole in the floor of the trunk where the spare tire would normally go. But I was happy either way. This was my car. There were even a few holes on the floorboard of the driver's side by the gas and brake pedals. I felt like the Flintstones whenever I drove that thing. Nonetheless, it was my own car that I had worked so hard and saved so much for. Well, a whopping six hundred dollars and, believe me, you could tell that it was worth every dollar. Hell, I probably paid too much for it.

I quickly jumped onto the driver's seat and just held on to the steering wheel as though I had never seen something so magnificent. I was in heaven at that moment. I relished it well and am surprised to still remember it now as though it took place yesterday. I quickly looked over the dashboard and its instrument panel. I saw right away and acknowledged what would be the first thing I would buy for this awesome beast of a car, a stereo with cassette tape and some speakers. Never mind the torn seat that I was currently sitting on; I needed a good stereo that could play all my favorite cassette tapes. I'm old, I know. The back seat was just as bad, and it needed to be cleaned out. The car was filthy.

My grandfather quickly jumped onto the passenger side and asked me what I thought. "I love it!" I exclaimed. Then he asked me to turn it on and to take him out for a spin. My grandmother was way too frail by then and could not join us. I looked at her sitting outside on the porch of the house, and I waved goodbye at her as I cranked the car into life. I revved the car up a few times just to hear the engine roar, and I could see that my grandfather was just as ecstatic as I was. The big, old grin on his wrinkled face with his heavy glasses on just made the moment that much sweeter. Then just as we were both relishing the moment, a huge cloud of smoke made its way in through the open windows, and both of us began choking, first because of the smoke, and then we just continued choking with laughter over the whole ordeal. We were both enjoying something that was clearly not as great as we were making it out to be. I think the realization just made us laugh even more.

I placed the car in reverse and backed it out ever so slowly. I drove my grandfather around for about thirty minutes, and I quite honestly can't remember the route we took or even where we went. I was drunk in the moment of driving my very own car with my happy grandfather at my side. I think we both were. What I do recall is that we drove with the windows down and my grandfather asked me several times how the car felt and even told me a few times to really step on the gas so that we could see what the car had for power. It was a ride that I will always cherish. All those years of picking crops out in the hundred-degree weather didn't matter anymore. I was working outside the fields now, and I had my own car. The things I was striving for were coming to fruition, and I couldn't be happier.

Throughout the drive, I kept thinking back to all those days in the fields. The cold, wet mornings of October whenever we were picking tomatoes in Michigan and Ohio. How I would pray so much for the sun to rise faster so that I wouldn't be cold anymore. The aches and pains on my back and legs as we pushed through the hot temperatures, only to be making less than half of the country's minimum wage. Those were days of pain and misery. As I reminisced on those things throughout the drive, I felt proud of my accomplishments. I had gone against the grain, against the family, and done the unthinkable in order to begin my journey toward a better life. I had never felt as free as I did during that drive. I would look over toward my grandfather and see him smiling as well. I never asked him what he was thinking. I didn't want to. I just wanted to enjoy seeing him happy and proud; yes, I think he looked proud as well.

Upon returning to the house, my grandfather exited the car along with me, and then he walked cautiously around the car toward me. I thought he was going to show me something else on the car, ask me to pop the hood open, or give me a safety speech, as well as a sermon, on how owning a car is a great responsibility. He did none of those things. He simply continued to walk slowly toward me until he reached me and hugged me. It was a bear hug of sorts. I mean my grandfather truly put some strength into that hug and just held me there for a few moments. Maybe he had finally seen or understood what I was trying to do. What I was wanting to do with my life. I think that, maybe for the first time, he saw me as a man and he wanted to share his feelings with me. I hugged him back and held on to him like only a father and a son can hold on to each other. It was great.

That evening, my grandfather allowed me to enjoy the occasion without bringing up the topic of insurance and registration for the car. I couldn't get the registration under my name as a minor and without insurance. I couldn't get insurance on my own because I was a minor as well, and my grandfather was not budging at all on this matter. It took me a few days of arguing back and forth with my grandfather to realize that I was not going to convince him to help me out on this.

When my eighteenth birthday came around, I once again asked the neighbor next door for a ride to the testing site and if I could actually use his car for the driving portion of the test. The neighbor was happy to help, as always. At the testing facility, I lucked out because, after having passed the written portion, a female officer asked if I would be taking the driving portion that day as well. I stated that I was and handed over the vehicle's insurance and registration paperwork.

That lady must have been desperate or something because, when I say I lucked out, I mean I lucked out. She sat on the passenger seat and asked me to turn the car on. She then proceeded to give me instructions on what roads to take and which turns to make. I followed all the traffic signs throughout the exam and really didn't pay much attention to the officer. When it became time to do the parallel-parking portion, she looked at me, smiled, and said that I didn't need to do that portion of the exam. I don't know if she was expecting me to do something in return, but she didn't get anything. I took the car right back to the testing facility and got off as quick as possible. She had no choice but to follow suit and hand over the results of my driving exam to the front desk. The secretary at the front desk smiled at me and said, "Congratulations, you passed."

I was so excited that I took my paper driver's license and rushed out of there without even thanking the officer who had given me the driving portion of the exam. I ran outside toward my neighbor and showed him my brand-new driver's license. I was legal to drive now, well, with the exception of the whole insurance deal, of course.

I remember my neighbor dropping me off at school after the driving exam. I asked him to please inform my grandparents that I had passed and thanked him for letting me use his car once again. Once in class, I began to think of the issues I had to deal with, insurance and vehicle registration. It had already been made clear that the registration would need to be entirely under my name and that I would also need to purchase insurance for my car. I just didn't know how I would pull it off exactly or if I could even afford it with the money I was making at the restaurant. I could not afford to skip any bills at home in order to get everything done for the car; otherwise, I would never hear the end of it.

Luckily, I was in computer science at school and had access to computers. One morning, I went into my grandfather's Ford pickup and took his insurance with me. I walked over to the bus stop and studied the insurance card on the way to school. While in computer science class, I began typing up an exact replica of the insurance card with both my grandfather's name and mine. Once it was to my satisfaction, I printed it out, and the whole insurance matter was over.

With regard to the registration, back then a vehicle would be registered, and then two small decals were given to the registered owner. One of the decals would contain the month abbreviation, and the other decal contained the last two digits of the year for when it was due again. These two decals would be placed on the top corners of the vehicle's rear license plate. Needless to say, it was very easy for me to pull over at a local grocery store and acquire my vehicle registration off someone else's vehicle.

The only thing I had pending was the state inspection sticker for the car. Once that was complete, the vehicle would be ready to operate on the open road. I was fortunate enough at that time to have a classmate whose father worked at a shop where vehicle state inspections were done and had access to the inspection stickers. My friend charged me ten dollars, and I now had an inspection sticker for the car.

At home, my grandparents didn't really ask me any questions as to how I was able to get the car registered, insured, and inspected so quickly. They didn't ask for any paperwork or proof showing that I could legally drive the car. As I was the club president of the law enforcement club in school and then ultimately ended up with a career in law enforcement years later, it is funny and scary to remember a time when I was driving as illegal as could be. I can tell you now that, at this day and age, I would not approve of this course of action at all from any of my kids. Proof of legitimacy will be sought when their time comes.

Driving the car to school for the first time was such a great feeling. I'm sure that so many other students looked at it and told themselves that they wouldn't be caught dead in it, but not me. I was as happy as a pig in shit. I could not be prouder of my accomplishments, setting aside the whole legality of the vehicle registration, of course. It was as though I were the big man in campus, yet I was not a well-known student at all. Yet I knew I had paid for my own car with my own money as a senior in high school. I didn't have to rely on my parents for additional money, nor did I have to burden them further by incurring additional debt only to get me a car. I had done it all on my own, with my own sweat. I had so much to be proud of, and I was.

My dad (grandfather) and I at my mother's house in Reynosa, Mexico.

Senior Year

. . . .

Having the car enabled me to look for that second job. A friend of mine was able to square me away with a job as a stocker at Pop-A-Top, a local beer and liquor store. This was definitely a good thing because it allowed me to pay all the bills, buy groceries, and still have enough left over for my senior-year expenses at school. I had ensured to never again have to work in the fields and I couldn't be happier.

I remember having to show up to an interview for the job. An interview to stock beer? I felt the same way back then, yet I didn't let it bother me much since I needed the second job. The interview was conducted by a chubby fellow who must have been about twenty-five years old. I remember being asked if I drank beer; the answer was no. "Do you drink anything at all?" Once again, my answer was no. The chubby man laughed and asked me what type of Mexican I was. I didn't really have an answer for him other than I didn't drink and had never had the urge to do so. His last question to me was "If I say that you must know how every beer in here tastes like, would you drink from all of them to be able to answer questions about the different beers?" I knew this was a tough question, but I didn't know if my answer would determine my acceptance for the job. I was nervous, yet looked at the man with clear determination and said, "No."

He looked at me and said, "That's good, don't ever let anyone bully you into drinking or doing anything else that you don't feel comfortable with." After that quick two-minute interview, he took me around the store and showed me where everything was. Then we went to the back of the store, and he began showing me how to make six-packs of beer cans with the thin plastic holders. He gave me a chance to try it, and once he saw that I could manage it, he asked me if I could start that Friday. I was excited and said yes right away. I did inform him of my job as a waiter at the Chinese restaurant and that I would need to start work at his store at eleven o'clock at night since we would close the restaurant at ten. The chubby fellow shook my hand, welcomed me to the Pop-A-Top family, and said it would be okay.

My senior year of high school was off to a great start. I was able to save enough for a car, had been able to land two jobs that would help out the entire household, and most importantly, I had guaranteed to not have to work in the fields anymore. I didn't see any downside to how I had arranged my school-to-work schedule. After the first week of attending classes and having to work both jobs, I realized how tiring the entire ordeal actually was. I wasn't getting enough sleep since I still had to take care of homework after my second job. I remember having to be awake until about three in the morning, finishing up most of my homework and then having to get up early enough to finish it prior to going to school.

I think my grandparents could see how grueling my schedule was but for some reason were not saying anything. Maybe they felt that my determination to stay out of the fields and make this schedule work for me was strong enough to make me ignore whatever they had to say about it. They were correct in that respect, if it was what they were thinking. I was truly determined to make it all work without it affecting my studies. Throughout the first month or so, my motivation was able to help push me through the rough schedule. But then, winter came, and with it came all those retired individuals from Canada and the northern states because of the warmer climate in South Texas. This meant more work for me at the restaurant and at the beer store.

I was probably about 130 pounds soaking wet back then. This extra work eventually began having an effect on me. I wasn't recovering as fast from my exhaustion and the lack of sleep I was experiencing every night. To make matters worse, my grandmother was losing her battle with cancer, and the doctors were telling us that she only had another month of life before she passed. This news was given to us in early November of 1992. Needless to say, nobody in the family was taking this well. I remember that final month clearly and can say that I would push myself to work harder and longer hours just so that I wouldn't have to see my grandmother in her weakened condition. I just didn't want to remember her in such a frail state. I wanted to remember the strong, hardworking old lady that I grew up with. The same old lady that would discipline me whenever I did something wrong or daring. I say daring because I was always pushing my own limitations as a kid. For some reason, I could never accept the words "You can't do that, you're too little or too skinny."

I think my grandmother loved that about me but still did her best to keep me in check whenever I got too daring. One occasion that comes to mind is my flying stunt in Mexico. When I was about nine years old, I had been taken to Reynosa, Mexico, to visit my mother for the weekend. She used to live in an apartment on the second floor. That apartment happened to have a balcony. All my life I have been a great fan of the superhero character Superman.

Well, on a glorious, sunny morning, I was ranting and raving to my mother and her sister about how awesome it would be to fly and be able to have your cape flapping behind you as you flew through the skies. My mother and aunt didn't waste any time at all and grabbed a towel, pinned it around my neck with a clothespin, and their little Superman was born. I must have run up and down the balcony steps a hundred times just so I could try and see the towel flapping behind me. This, of course, was a bit dangerous since I wasn't paying that much attention to the steps I was taking while trying to observe the towel behind me.

On one of my runs downstairs, I noticed an old bed mattress waiting to be picked up by the trash collector, who happened to be an old man and a donkey pulling a trailer. The craziest idea entered my mind, and I just ran with it. No hesitation on my part at all. I quickly grabbed the mattress and dragged it near the area just below my mother's balcony.

I ran upstairs again, extremely excited and overjoyed. Once on top, I climbed over the balcony railing, made sure I was directly above the mattress, took a deep breath, and jumped.

Once I landed, I was a bit disappointed because I completely forgot to look back and see if my makeshift cape was flapping in the air. So I ran upstairs and went through all the same steps, except this time I double-checked my position above the mattress and jumped with my head turned slightly to the side so that I could see the towel behind me. I landed on the mattress awkwardly and slid off it onto the paved sidewalk.

A lady from across the street actually saw me jump the second time and quickly ran out of her house, screaming at the top of her lungs for my mother, "Rosa! Rosa!" Suspecting that this lady was going to ruin my fun, I quickly got up and ran back upstairs toward the balcony. While at the top, I looked toward the door to my mother's apartment and saw that nobody was coming out. I once again climbed over the balcony onto the edge. The lady was at the bottom by the mattress, still yelling like there was no tomorrow. "No brinques! No brinques!" Don't jump! Don't jump!

I remember smiling at the lady and placing my index finger in front of my mouth, signaling her to be quiet. She must have gone into shock at that very moment because the look on her face was priceless, yet I was not going to be denied another jump. It was then that I heard my mother yelling behind me as well. I turned back to look at her and simply let go of the railing. That last jump was probably my best jump with the chaos created by the lady and my mother running to see if I had landed okay without being hurt. The beating that came after was well worth it.

One must remember that I was visiting my mother in Reynosa, Mexico, during this awesome flying experience. The downside to being raised by my grandparents was that, whenever I did get punished for something stupid, I would be punished by both my grandparents and my mother.

That day, I took my beating like the little Superman I was trying so hard to be. I honestly don't think I felt a thing, because I was still on my high from the jump. A few hours later when my grandparents showed up to pick me up, the second beating ensued, and it was horrible.

I remember sitting quietly in my mother's bedroom, and I didn't want to come out to see my grandparents. I knew they were discussing the events from that morning. I knew my fate was sealed and that there was no escaping it. Finally, my grandmother called me out of the bedroom and told me to go stand next to her. If I was breathing at that moment, I don't remember. The fear of what was coming was overwhelming. I made my way toward my grandmother, which was probably about fifteen steps at the most, but it sure felt like I was walking a hundred yards or more. I stood in front of her and just kept looking down at my own feet because I knew the wrath in her eyes would burn straight through me.

The only words I heard were "Juan, dame la faja." John, give me the belt. I just stood there, afraid to even breathe, paralyzed. My grandfather removed his belt and handed it over to my grandmother. I clenched my hands and shut my eyes, anticipating the first strike. When it finally came down on the back of my legs, I jumped up in pain and lost all composure. I was crying bloody murder as I took on three or four more strikes with the belt. After she was done, she demanded that I stop crying and stand straight. How could I? I was in pain. Then, I heard her say the famous Mexican phrase that continues to be used today whenever a kid is being punished, "Para que aprendas!" That way you'll learn!

I learned, all right. I never jumped off the balcony or anything else again, well, until I joined the military, of course.

My grandmother passed away on December 5, 1992. The speed in which my senior year of high school had kicked off with slowed down to a crawl after that day. I felt lost and truly didn't know how to continue moving forward with my studies and my jobs. I eventually quit my job at Pop-A-Top in order to make more time for my studies and to just be home with my grandfather.

All their kids had married and left the house already, so we were the only two left along with my cousin Hilda. The days and the nights dragged on for the first week after my grandmother's passing. December 12 is known as a feast day in the United States and better known by Catholics as the date of celebrating or honoring Our Lady of Guadalupe, the Patroness of the Americas.

At the beginning of my senior year, I had joined the school's folk-dancing class, and our first performance of the year was to be at the very church where we held my grandmother's services, St. Pius X Catholic Church of Weslaco, Texas. I had already been excused by my dancing teacher to not participate in the dance and celebration for that evening, but the decision to do so was not even mine to make.

Before my grandmother passed away, she would always ask me how my folk-dancing practices were going. She would also tell me constantly not to worry and that she would make it to my first performance since it was in honor of Our Lady of Guadalupe. Thus, when my teacher informed me that it was okay for me to not perform because of my grandmother's passing, I thanked her and told her that I would still be dancing that day. My grandmother had looked forward to that day for several months, and there was no way I was going to disappoint her.

I remember addressing this issue with my grandfather and my mother. I told them how strongly I felt about performing, that it was my grandmother's wish. They, along with the entire family, obliged and said that they would all attend to honor my grandmother's wish.

I remember that evening vividly. I was a nervous wreck for two reasons: one, it was our first public performance, and two, I knew how much this performance had meant to my grandmother, and I didn't want to disappoint her. Now, up to this point, I had never been one to believe in mysterious things such as apparitions. My grandmother had always told me stories of how she had seen ghosts in her lifetime and how they do exist. I would always laugh it off and tell her that the stories were interesting but hard to believe. So in her own way, my grandmother would always laugh with me as well while telling me that one day she would prove to me that such beings existed.

Something strange occurred that evening of December 12, 1992. I was not able to greet my family when they walked into the church and took their seats, and I didn't get to see them until I was already performing on the makeshift stage that had been built for the night's celebration. As I performed our various dances in honor of Our Lady of Guadalupe, I was able to see that my family had been seated in the front row. What was strange to me about their seats is that for some reason they had left an empty seat next to my grandfather.

I remember dancing the first two pieces and all of a sudden becoming overwhelmed with emotion backstage as we were prepping for the next number. I can only assume that my teacher and my classmates noticed this because they all began asking me if I was okay or telling me that it was okay for me to step down and not perform.

To this day, I can't explain the immense emotion that overcame me or why it had hit me so suddenly during my performance. I told everyone that I was okay and made an attempt to regain my composure for the next number. I remember stepping onto that stage and staring blankly at the empty chair next to my grandfather, wondering why my family had chosen to skip a chair.

The music began to play, and the performance began. With every turn or spin that I took throughout that performance, I would always glance over to that chair, which I believe only caused my emotions to get the best of me. Somewhere around midperformance, I saw something that has baffled me to this day; my grandmother was sitting next to my grandfather, watching me perform.

It may have been the overwhelming emotions and sensation of the whole reason behind this particular performance, but I swear I could see her clearly looking at me dance with a smile on her face. I was in a trance for the rest of the song and tried my best to control my tears and hold on to my fake smile. As soon as the song ended and we all bowed to the audience, we exited behind the curtains again, and I just collapsed, crying.

One of my classmates quickly came to my aid and assisted me back up. I remember telling my classmate what I had just experienced, and the look on his face was a mix between astonishment and confusion. He made the call immediately. I was not to perform anymore that night. A few moments later, our teacher came over and asked me if everything was okay. Of course it wasn't; I simply explained to her that my emotions were getting the best of me and I would not be able to perform anymore that night. Luckily, she agreed and allowed me to sit out.

After the show was over, we all went out to meet and greet the audience. I went over to my family and hugged them all. I remember telling my mother and grandfather that one of my classmates was going to take me home later on after we cleaned up and took everything back to the school.

Upon my arrival at the house, both my mother and grandfather were waiting up for me. I can only assume that the expression on my face told them that something was not quite all right, and so they asked what was wrong. I sat down and told them what I had experienced during my last performance that night. My mother began to cry and couldn't really tell me why an empty chair had been left next to my grandfather. She said it wasn't anything they intended to do; it was just something that happened with no reason whatsoever.

My grandfather, on the other hand, gave me a big hug and held me tight. After his embrace, he looked at me with tears in his eyes and a great, big smile. I remember the words he told me afterward so vividly, "Tu abuela te había dicho que un día te iba hacer creer en esas cosas que ella te decia. Tambien te habia dicho todos estos meses que ella iba ver tu primer presentacion de baile." Your grandmother had told you that one day she would make a believer out of you about all those stories she used to tell you. She had also told you all these months that she would see your first dance performance. As soon as he was done telling me this, the three of us just looked at each other, crying and accepting that my grandmother had kept her promise even after her death. I had never been a believer of the supernatural until that night. I don't know what caused me to see her on that chair; I just know I did.

A few months later, my grandfather and I were the only ones living in our house. My cousin had moved out because the memory of our grandmother was too much for her to bear. My mother believed that my grandfather and I were experiencing a more severe form of depression. I had quit my job at the beer and liquor store so that I could dedicate more time to my schoolwork and mostly to just have more time to myself.

One weekend while visiting my mother in Reynosa, Mexico, she informed me that she had hired a witch doctor to help us with our depression. At first I began to laugh at the idea, and once I saw how my mother reacted to my laughter, I got a bit more serious and asked her if she truly believed that was what I needed and if she truly believed in such things as healers or *curanderos*, who are more commonly known as witch doctors. The look on my mother's face was all the answer I needed to know exactly how serious of a matter this was for her.

She began expressing how much she worried about my grandfather and I and how the death of my grandmother had somehow affected the two of us more than it had affected anyone else in the family. I tried explaining to her that it wasn't the case at all and that we just needed to figure out how to spend our time now that we didn't have to care for my grandmother. So much of our time had been consumed by her illness that we were having a hard time adjusting to all the free time we now had. After a few minutes of discussion, I realized my mother was not going to budge on the whole witch-doctor ordeal. My grandfather and I both agreed to be "cleansed" by the witch doctor if only to at least help my mother feel at ease.

Once we gave her the okay, she quickly got on the phone and called the witch doctor to make arrangements. We were only visiting for the weekend, so it needed to happen that Saturday or early Sunday. Arrangements were made for Sunday morning. I was trying to not make light of the whole witch-doctor deal, but I just couldn't resist asking my mother if we needed to fast before our medical appointment. The scornful look she gave me was all I needed to realize that this was a serious matter for her.

So Sunday morning came around, and we all waited patiently for the witch doctor to show up after breakfast. The lady didn't show up until about eleven o'clock that morning, but once she got there, things got a bit too dramatic for my taste. The lady must have been close to seventy years old, had long grayed-out hair, and barely had any teeth left. I remember answering the knocking on the door, and I had to take a step back upon seeing her for the first time. She announced who she was and asked for my mother. For some strange reason, I hesitated for a moment that was long enough for my mother to interject and let the old witch doctor into the house.

She walked in carrying a large satchel with her, and she appeared to be holding on to it as though her life depended on it or as if she were keeping something very powerful away from us. Her clothes were indigenous at best, yet they gave her a strange, macabre sort of look, maybe because of how ragged they looked or just her overall appearance in general. She did have a very stern look about her as she stood in our small living room, listening to my mother explain what she believed was going on with my grandfather and me. As my mother continued with her explanation of the past month's events, I noticed that the old lady would not sit down, would not touch anything at all in the house. I had offered her a glass of water, and she shushed it away as though I had somehow presented a deadly item to her or had somehow disrupted her concentration. After my mother completed her explanation of events, the old lady scanned the entire living room as though she were scanning a huge building, when the living room was only a ten-by-ten. She directed us to move all the furniture away from the center of the room so that she could have space to work with. My grandfather and I quickly moved our furniture around. There wasn't much to move, just a small couch, two small chairs, and a coffee table. She then took a close look at my grandfather and me; my guess is she was trying to see or decide whom to start off with. She chose my grandfather.

My grandfather was directed to stand in the center of the room. I stood near one of the corners and remained extremely vigilant of what was taking place. I wanted to see everything this old lady was doing. I just didn't believe in these things and wanted to see if I could catch something deceitful.

As my grandfather took his place in the center of the room, the old lady went digging into her satchel and pulled out a small vial with a clear liquid in it. She immediately commenced to reciting a strange chant using a language that I could not understand. It wasn't Spanish, and my only guess now is that it must have been in her native tongue.

She then took the vial of liquid and poured it onto the floor, forming a circle around my grandfather as she continued with her chant. I noticed my mother standing against one of the walls with a rosary in hand as she recited her own prayers. After the ring was formed around my grandfather, the old lady went back into her satchel and pulled out a thick wad of weeds. The chant continued. She signaled to my grandfather to extend his arms to his sides, and as he did, the old lady began slapping his body with the weeds.

My grandfather had closed his eyes, so I truly couldn't read his expression as the weeds kept on being slapped against him; he was deep into the whole ritual himself. The old lady walked around my grandfather and outside the ring of fluid she had poured on the floor, slapping him everywhere with those weeds as her chant continued.

I remember seeing her actually slap him on the face with them and thinking, *That old witch is not going to slap the shit out of me!* It had looked painful, and it sounded horrible as the weeds came across my grandfather's face.

The old lady suddenly threw the wad of weeds away from my grandfather, and her chant grew louder and louder as though she were reaching the grand finale or something. Then all of a sudden, silence. She stopped her chant and raised her hands in the air, and out of nowhere, she had pulled out a box of matches, which I could now see in one of her hands. I remember thinking and trying to convince myself that she had to have had them hidden inside that wad of weeds because she hadn't gone back to her satchel a third time. I saw her light up a match and dropped it on the ring of liquid around my grandfather.

The entire ring lit up in flames around him, and she began her chant again, only this time she was wailing as she waved her hands near and around my grandfather and once again raising the pitch of her voice louder and louder until she reached her starting point and once again, silence. The old lady looked down at the ring of fire and sort of grinned with a sense of satisfaction. She instructed my grandfather to open his eyes and look at her as she addressed him, "Mire usted este anillo de lumbre. Su limpieza a sido todo un exito. Lo e curado de todas sus inseguridades y ahora puede seguir su vida tranquilo." Look at this ring of fire. Your cleansing has been a success. I have cured you of all your insecurities, and you may now continue living life peacefully. My grandfather thanked her as he remained inside the ring of fire.

The old lady then instructed me to get a mop and a bucket of water so that she could clean the floor before my cleansing began. I obeyed my instruction and quickly brought her a bucket of water and a mop. My mother offered to grab the mop, but the old lady quickly slapped her hands away. "Tu no puedes intervenir en esto. Yo tengo que hacer todo para que esto funcione." You can't interfere in this. I must do everything in order for this to work. My mother shied away from the old lady and allowed her to continue. The old lady grabbed the mop, doused it in water, and then began to mop the ring of fire around my grandfather until all the fire had been put out. Once she was content that the floor was clean, she instructed my grandfather to step away and looked at me, letting me know that it was my turn.

I set the mop and bucket of water to the side and took my place in the center of the room. She went back to her satchel and pulled out the same little vial of fluid and poured it on the floor, forming a ring around me just as she had done with my grandfather. Having initiated her chant again, I remember thinking that I could not bear to listen to that chant much longer.

Once the ring was in place around me, she went back to her satchel and dug up another wad of weeds, except this time, I paid close attention to her hands and saw that she was already holding the box of matches. I extended my arms when told to do so, just like my grandfather before me did, as she began to slap the wad of weeds against me. Now that I was the center of her ritual, I can attest to the fact that she wasn't just slapping the weeds against me in a soft manner. No, she was literally slapping the crap out of me with those things.

I took it and kept my eyes on her the entire time although, I must say, that it was tough to do once she began slapping my face. I was forced to close my eyes; that crap was unbearable, and to this day I don't know how my grandfather took it without even reacting. She once again flung the wad of weeds away from me when she was done slapping me and raised her hands in the air as her chant grew louder.

Then something different took place. I saw her light up the match and drop it onto the ring around me. The ring began to burst with flames around me, but it didn't complete the whole circle. I did not have a complete ring of fire around me. Something had gone wrong. She looked down at the floor, puzzled, and didn't begin her chant again as she had done with my grandfather. Then she looked at me in a mean way, as though I had done something for the ring to not light up completely.

Needless to say, I smiled.

The old lady backed away from me and began speaking to all of us in Spanish again, "Su hijo tiene algo muy mal por dentro. Esto nunca a sucedido. Yo me tengo que ir de aquí." Your son has something bad inside of him. This has never happened. I have to leave this place.

After making this declaration, the old lady quickly began getting all her things back into the satchel and didn't even bother to give us an explanation or let my mother pay her for her services. I stepped out of the half ring and tried telling my mother to let the old lady leave, she was more than likely a fake, and all this was just an act to get more money from us down the road. "Pero te tiene que aliviar, mijo." But she has to cure you, son. I was already of the mind that this old lady would say that she would have to do a different ritual, which required more things and, of course, would be more expensive. My mother was not seeing it that way. She just wanted me "cured."

That old lady grabbed her things and walked out of the house at such a fast pace for her age, and she never looked back. The three of us were left standing there, perplexed at the events that had just taken place. My poor mother and grandfather had this look of concern or fear because the old lady had said that there was something bad inside me.

I couldn't help but start laughing and telling them that this was all an act and to not believe what the old lady was saying. I grabbed the mop and began mopping the half ring of fire and the rest of the space around it. My mother and grandfather just stood there looking at me trying to figure out why I wasn't worried at all. After I finished, I once again reminded them that I didn't believe in that stuff and that they shouldn't worry about me. I don't think I was too convincing, but then again, what choice did they have? I finished my senior year of high school without any other major incidents. I continued working as a waiter at Red Peppers. Attended some of the local school events just like most of my classmates and somehow still ended up in the top

10 percent of my class. My graduating class was probably about 648 students.

Probably about a month or two before graduating, I walked into an army recruiting office and enlisted. In my mind, I was keeping my promise to my grandmother by not enlisting in the Marines. Whether she sees it that way or not will be known down the line when my time comes to leave this earth.

Folk dancing outside a shopping center in Weslaco, Texas.

Fort Knox, Kentucky

· · · · · · · · · · · · · · · · · · ·

I went through the Army Basic Training at Fort Knox, Kentucky. One must keep in mind that, when I joined the military, I was clueless as to what a military career entailed. I didn't have anyone at home who knew anything about the military other than what was seen on television. My grandparents had originally kept me from enlisting because they still believed that all the crap they had seen during the Vietnam era was also taking place in 1992. I had no uncles or cousins who had joined who could tell me a thing or two about what to expect. I simply walked in blindly. The first time I ever flew on a plane was to fly over to Kentucky from San Antonio, Texas. I was nervous, to say the least. To make matters worse, I was pretty shy because of my poor English-speaking skills.

I would read every single sign I saw and somehow managed to figure out my way through the airport to my actual gate without incident. I remember seeing everyone else walking around with books in their hands, newspapers, and the younger folks walking around with portable cassette players and headphones.

At first I wondered why people were doing this; we were, after all, just going to get on a plane and travel somewhere. It wasn't until I had to take a seat at my flight's assigned gate that I realized how much better the trip would be if I did have a portable cassette player or Walkman to be able to listen to some music and, hopefully, relax.

Although I was intrigued and somewhat excited with everything I was observing, I was still a nervous mess. I say *cassette player* because of how poor and clueless I actually was about the latest technology at that time. Compact disks (CDs) were already out, but owning one never even crossed my mind as a possibility, at least not in my current financial situation.

Having been raised the way I was and having lived in the conditions I lived, my new surroundings at the airport in San Antonio, Texas, truly made me feel uncomfortable. Not necessarily because it was all new to me, but because it all somehow made me feel like an outsider. It was as if I didn't belong there at all, and this feeling only added to my nervousness.

What was I doing there? What the hell was I going to do in the military? And more importantly, what the hell was I thinking? I wasn't sure of anything at that point. I didn't know what to expect, how I was supposed to act or behave, and far more worrisome was the fact that I truly didn't know whom I was supposed to meet with once I landed in Kentucky.

All the other recruits who had just enlisted along with me didn't seem to be as nervous as I was. At least that was what I thought at that time. All we had been told at the Military Entrance Processing Station (MEPS) was that someone in uniform would show up to the airport in a shuttle and for us to report directly to that individual. Said individual would in turn take us all to our designated "welcoming" facility on base.

It was made quite clear later on that their definition of "welcoming" differed a whole lot from mine.

Well, I boarded my plane and flew on over to Kentucky. The takeoff was fairly exciting and scary at once. Throughout the flight, all I could think about was wondering what things would be like at my destination. What to expect and, more importantly, do what I must in order to complete whatever training I was about to get put through. These thoughts just intensified my already-nervous state.

Although I'm sure I had my family's thoughts and prayers, I felt all alone. This was my first time venturing away from home without the presence or even the thought of being able to lean on family for support and guidance. Had I made the right decision? Back then, I wasn't too confident that I had made the right decision. Now, I know I did.

The landing was a bit unexpected yet fine nonetheless. I remember thinking that flying wasn't bad at all, and I had actually liked my first experience. As people around me began to gather their things once the plane stopped, I began to worry about not linking up with the appropriate person who would take me to the base. I began looking around me, frantically trying to spot other nervous young men such as myself. I wanted confirmation that I wasn't the only one in this situation, and I wanted to find someone I could follow to the correct pickup spot.

At that moment, I think I still believed that I was the only person on the plane who had never flown before. This careless thought somehow reassured me that finding another "lost" individual would somehow ease my own fears. I spotted a guy, and he must have been doing the same thing I was doing, because he looked just as nervous, and we both somehow just knew that we would link up in the airport and somehow find our way to the appropriate army personnel.

I'll be honest in saying that I can't even remember the individual's name. I can say that we both linked up after we got off the plane, confirmed with each other that we were both headed to Fort Knox for basic training, and began making our way to the baggage claim area.

After getting our bags, we made our way out toward the main exit, departures area, and immediately saw a soldier waiting by the doorway with a sign that read, "Fort Knox—Basic Training." We made our way to the soldier, a specialist, and introduced ourselves. Asked him about the shuttle for Fort Knox, and he guided us outside to a small old gray school bus.

The specialist told us to get in and to place our bags on our laps. As more recruits boarded the bus, it was clear that the bags we were all carrying were just way too much for the instructions given to us. About fifteen minutes later, the specialist jumped into the bus and tells us all in a stern voice that we must make room for two people in each seat.

I was carrying an old, beat-up suitcase and an oversized gym bag. Once I placed both items on my lap, I couldn't see anything in front of me. I could look over to my left since I had taken a window seat on the right side of the bus, but even that bit of vision was cut off the moment another guy sat next to me. His bags were bigger than mine, and there was barely any wiggle room between us and all the bags that all I could do was turn toward the window and look out. To make matters worse, the temperature inside the bus began getting hot as hell being overcrowded with young men and luggage. I could only imagine how everyone else was doing. Me, I was burning up; this was the month of June, after all.

As uncomfortable as we all were sitting inside that bus, nobody said anything, nobody gasped or sighed heavily, the silence on that bus was deafening. Some time passed when I heard the specialist's voice again over all the luggage surrounding me.

"Are all the seats filled?" he asked as the heavy sound of his footsteps made its way toward the back of the bus and back to the front. "Well then, you six will have to stand in the center aisle with all your bags. You guys are lucky, you don't have to place your luggage on your lap." This statement was followed by more footsteps onto the bus and grunts of other young men trying to walk through the center aisle with all their crap. How they were lucky, I don't know. Shortly after, the bus began rolling away from the airport.

The ride toward the base was uneventful and as quiet as could be. I think we were all just scared out of our minds, not knowing exactly what to expect once we arrived. At least for me, that was the case. It was already dark when we arrived. I couldn't even move my hand so that I could see what time it was. Once the bus came to a complete stop at our destination, another man got on the bus and began yelling immediately, "Get off my bus, ladies, and get your asses into the building directly in front of you. Now hurry the fuck up, get off my bus, and leave all your shit on the wall outside the building!" At that moment, I thought the madness had begun; man, was I ever so wrong.

I think all of us moved at once, and that only added to the chaos even more. Those of us in the seats were trying to get out while all those standing in the aisle were still in our way. We were all hitting one another with our luggage, trying to get off the bus in frantic fashion.

Outside the bus were several drill sergeants yelling at the top of their lungs for us to hurry up because we were moving too slow for them. Some guys were dropping their bags accidentally as they were getting off the bus, and the drill sergeants would just kick the bags away from them and yell some more while others actually grabbed the bags and threw them against the wall.

At the door of the building was another drill sergeant yelling at us to drop our shit and take a seat inside. Walking into the room was like hitting a heated wall. The room was so hot inside, and I later noticed that only about three windows were open with very little air coming through. Once everyone was seated inside, all the drill sergeants walked in, and one of them began to speak in what must have been the loudest voice I had ever heard.

"Stay awake, ladies. We have a lot of paperwork to fill out and no time to do it. If you feel like sleep is about to kick your ass, I suggest you fight that shit and stand up because, if we have to get your asses up, it will not be pretty."

The heat inside was rough, and I guess it was tougher on others because a bunch of guys took turns at standing up throughout the two hours or so that it took us to fill out all the paperwork. Me, I was raised without ever having an air-conditioning unit in the house. I even had to sleep on the floor by our screen door for many years just to cool off a bit throughout the night, so the heat wasn't that bad on me; I was used to it. That and fear of the drill sergeants kept me in check during that time.

Afterward, we were made to rush outside again, picked up our luggage, and then escorted to our temporary barracks in formation. By escorted I mean we were made to march in formation to our temporary barracks.

The three or four blocks we attempted to march toward those barracks were a nightmare. Trying to stay in line with all our luggage in hand was impossible, and things got even worse when some of us actually dropped one of our bags during the march. I don't think I had ever heard so much yelling and cursing in my life. At least at that point in time anyway.

I think my favorite one at the time was "What the hell are you doing to my formation, ladies? Are you all trying to make me look bad out here?"

I say it was my favorite because at that time I was actually wondering what the hell the drill sergeant was talking about. I kept shifting my eyes to both sides, and I couldn't see anyone else out there on the streets besides us. Thus, I kept asking myself, *Whom are we making him look bad in front of?*

The entire in-processing for basic training took one week. During that week, we were issued our uniforms, got our hair cut completely off, learned the basics of formations, marching, facing movements, and we were made to run everywhere. Anytime we were outside, if we were not engaged in doing something, we were running.

This was where I actually learned that I hate running.

After our in-processing was completed, we were all yelled at to get our shit together and board a bus that was taking us to our actual assigned companies for the beginning of our basic training. One early morning, we all crammed into a regular bus with all our luggage and now our duffel bags full of uniforms and issued equipment. Once again, nobody could see anything except the luggage sitting in front of us on the bus. Our drill sergeant boarded the bus and warned us about not making him and the rest of his cadre look bad once we arrived at our assigned company. Shortly after getting off, the bus began its slow drive toward Delta Company.

As soon as the bus came to a complete stop, the bus was immediately surrounded by about ten different drill sergeants. One of them boarded the bus, and all hell broke loose. "What the hell are you all still doing on my bus? Get the fuck off this bus now! Are you all waiting for an invitation?"

All of us must have jumped from our seats at once because luggage and duffel bags were flying all over the place, everyone was trying to run out of the bus, and we were all striking one another with our bags. We were all in panic mode, and having ten different drill sergeants yelling at us outside only made our situation that much more chaotic and stressful.

Duffel bags and suitcases were being snatched away from us and dropped on the ground because we weren't moving fast enough. "What are you doing just looking at me, Private? Do I look cute to you? Move your ass, now, now, now!"

I remember stepping off the bus and a thin, muscular drill sergeant Shep stopping me with the palm of his hands, taking a close look at my name tag, and yelling, "Private *Tinko* , what the fuck kind of name is that?"

I just stared blankly.

"Well, Private, are you going to answer my question or just stand there looking stupid?" I looked at his black face and, with the softest of voices, corrected him, "It's *Tinoco* [tee-no-ko], Drill Sergeant."

It was at that point that I learned to never again correct a drill sergeant. I didn't know any better then, but I sure did learn that lesson in a heartbeat.

"Did you just fucking correct me, Private? Are you telling me that I don't know how to fucking read? Well, let me tell you something, dumb shit. If I say your name is Private *Tinko*, you better believe it will be Private *Tinko* for the rest of your pathetic life! Do I make myself clear, shit for brains?"

I think I was going deaf at that moment because his face was so close to mine that his words were actually piercing through my ears. I thought he was about to eat me alive.

So once again in the softest of voices, I said, "Yes, Drill Sergeant."

"I can't hear you, Private *Tinko*!"

Now at the top of my lungs and in his face, I answered, "Yes, Drill Sergeant! I understand, Drill Sergeant!"

I truly believed he was about to whoop my ass for having yelled into his face. It couldn't be prevented, though; the man's face was literally an inch away from mine. I was not used to having conversations up close and personal like this.

"Then get the hell out of my face, Private. Move your ass, move, move, move!"

I immediately ran to the side, bumping into other privates and their bags as I tried to escape from that situation. Needless to say, I was Private *Tinko* every single day of basic training.

As we all ran into one another and continually dropped our bags, the drill sergeants continued their wrath of yelling and cursing at us. They made us run up to the front of what would be our barracks and had us form up. Through the yelling, we were instructed to listen for our names and platoon. Our platoons were Alpha, Bravo, Charlie, and Delta. We were supposed to line up in formation in our assigned platoons.

The chaos continued as our names were called out rapidly, making it more difficult to actually hear which platoon we were assigned to. After about five minutes of this, all four platoons were formed up. Then the drill sergeants standing in front of our platoons began calling out our names again to do a roll call and ensure we were in the correct formation. Those of us who were not in our assigned formation were dealt with harshly.

"Do you not understand fucking English, Private? What the hell are you doing in that platoon over there? Are you telling me my platoon is not good enough for you?"

It didn't help that all four drill sergeants were yelling out our names simultaneously and all the other drill sergeants were yelling at us all this crap as well. It was madness at its best. Once again we were being forced to pay close attention for our names and which platoon we were supposed to be in while trying to ignore all the other crap that was being screamed at us.

After everyone was formed up in their respective platoons, the madness just got even worse. The drill sergeants told all their platoons which floor belonged to them. I was in Delta Platoon, and our assigned floor was the third floor of the barracks. Once we got our information, we were told to run upstairs with all our crap and find a bunk. We were to place our bags on top of a bunk and then run back down to hold formation again.

All four platoons were let go at once. The craziness of trying to fit through the entrance and then to go up three flights of stairs was unlike anything I had seen or experienced before. I want to say that there was no thinking involved at all, our bodies were just moving, and our minds were trying to push through the fear that was overwhelming us all. We could all hear the drill sergeants yelling all kinds of crap at us while we struggled and fought to make it all the way up, find an empty bunk, drop our bags, and then have to fight through the stairs again to get back down.

One thing was already clear: no matter what we did, we were not fast enough.

Throughout basic training, I had three drill sergeants. A black man, probably the meanest of all since he was our senior drill sergeant, was Sergeant First Class Shep. A Hispanic man who seemed to be the quietest yet craziest instructor was Staff Sergeant Rios. Lastly, we had a white man who didn't quite fit the picture of a drill sergeant because of his build, which made him look chubby; he was also a staff sergeant, named Ruff. All three men had a peculiar way of making our lives a living hell throughout basic.

Drill Sergeant Rios was the shortest of the three, and he always loved to challenge one of us to try to fight him. "You think you can take me, Private? Is that why you're eye-fucking me? Do you like me, or do you just want to have your way with me?" This guy was hilarious. The tougher he acted with us, the higher he jumped. It was as if jumping higher would make his point that much more serious.

Drill Sergeant Ruff would always challenge all of us in every exercise we ever did. None of us could ever keep up with him, much less beat him at it. He was the funniest of the three. I remember a few mornings when he would actually show up to our physical training (PT) sessions with a few cupcakes in his hands.

"All you pieces of shit think I'm fat anyway. Not to worry, Privates, I got something for that ass! Just let me finish my cupcakes, and we'll see who is able to survive this PT session! This here sugar just helps me out with my second wind, and you all better fucking pray that I don't catch my second wind towards the end, Privates! God help you if I do, because, if I do, we will be out here until I collapse!"

His shit was funny, but none of us would ever laugh, at least not in front of him or in formation. Hell, to be honest, I think we all just wanted a few cupcakes ourselves.

Drill Sergeant Shep, on the other hand, was all business. I don't think I ever saw him laugh or smile, and God help us if we didn't accomplish something to his standards. We would be made to PT all day and all night. Hell, he would sometimes call the drill sergeants from the other platoons so that they could take turns with us while he contemplated his next move or took a break from giving us hell.

The rest of basic training was pretty much the same. The first two weeks were the worst, though. We ran every single day, and the physical training was brutal. Push-ups and sit-ups for everything done incorrectly or not done fast enough, for not keeping up on the runs, and even for not sounding off loud enough.

I will say that we were taken to a military chapel every Sunday so that we could listen to an army chaplain give us a sermon. One particular Sunday, though, we were joined at the chapel by our company first sergeant. He walked into the chapel just before the chaplain began his sermon and addressed us all.

"Men, isn't this a glorious morning at Fort Knox?" "Yes, First Sergeant!"

"Men, I didn't hear you. I asked, isn't this a glorious morning to hear the Good Word at Fort Knox?"

"Yes, First Sergeant!"

"You men mean to tell me that you are not feeling the good spirit this morning? I ask this because I still can't hear you, and if I can't hear you—then the Good Lord sure as heck can't hear you!"

The first sergeant paced up and down the center of the chapel, looking at all of us with utter disgust and disappointment. He then turned over to the drill sergeants who had marched us over to the chapel and told them that we sounded sleepy and might need to be woken up properly before listening to the Good Word.

In an instant, the drill sergeants yelled out, "Formation outside, now!"

We all ran outside the chapel and formed up on its front lawn. We were given the half-right-facing command and then, "Front-leaning-rest position, MOVE!" We were about to be woken up.

As we all assumed the push-up position, we could all see the first sergeant standing behind our drill sergeants, looking at us. "Men, we are going to push this ground until we reach the other side of the earth or until I'm satisfied that you are all ready to receive the Good Word of the Lord! Now, PUSH!"

We did push-ups that morning until every last one of us began collapsing from the exhaustion, and then they switched us over on our backs and we began doing flutter kicks, crunches, reverse crunches, and abdominal twists until we couldn't do any more. But that wasn't enough though. According to the first sergeant that morning, we still weren't ready to receive the Good Word of the Lord, and we still hadn't pushed the ground down to the other side of the earth either.

I believe that this was the worst PT session of our entire basic training. By the time they got done with us, our uniforms were a mess, we were a mess, our faces and hands were full of dirt and sweat, and we could barely catch our breath or move. They kept us out there for about forty grueling minutes of nonstop physical training, and then the first sergeant said he believed we were ready to receive the Good Word of the Lord.

Once inside the chapel, I prayed and prayed and prayed some more. I don't think I even listened to a single word the chaplain said that morning. How could I? I was too exhausted to pay attention. I was completely lost in my own thoughts, prayers, and the excruciating pain

I was feeling. Every part of my body ached.

I will say this though; from that day on, we would sound-off so loud that the city of Louisville, Kentucky, could hear us. Sounding off was no longer an issue for my platoon, and going to the chapel was never the same.

The first two weeks of training were horrible for me. I guess that being a scrawny six-foot kid who had picked crops for a living by being bent over most of the time caused me to develop a poor posture. I could not stand straight to save my life. This was not a good thing when it came to formations and addressing the drill sergeants.

After a few times of yelling at me to straighten the hell up and not being able to do so, the drill sergeants began walking around with a thin metal rod that resembled a vehicle antenna. During formations, if I was not standing straight, one of the drill sergeants would simply strike me on the upper part of my back to force me to stand straight. That thing hurt like a bitch. I remember the first time I was struck with it; it came to me as a surprise, and it stung like hell.

"Straighten the fuck up, TINKO! You are standing at the position of attention, Private!"

And then the strike came. I arched my body in an attempt to straighten up and still couldn't manage to do so because I felt that medal rod strike my back again. I must have been struck about ten times that day. The number of strikes I received lessened as the days passed, but my back continued to hurt more and more as it got sore from all those hits.

By the end of the second week, I no longer had this issue. I would automatically assume the perfect position of attention with no hesitation. Their bullshit worked. Running everywhere and road marches were commonplace during basic training. One route that we all hated and feared was referred to as the Trinity Hills by our drill sergeants. It was a route of about twenty kilometers that consisted of three hills commonly and justifiably named Misery, Agony, and Heartbreak. Those hills were the cause of many new privates going home because they just couldn't complete the ruck march or the run; a few of them would just quit their training because of it.

I remember the first time we did the ruck march on that route. Going up Misery was bad; many of us were hurting and had to lean forward as much as possible to not allow the weight of the rucksack drag us down on the steep incline. Drill sergeants were yelling and cursing at us the entire way up, telling us how this was nothing and how we needed to prepare for far worse obstacles than that hill.

We didn't know it at that time, but when we reached the top of that hill we found out exactly what our drill sergeants were talking about. At the top of Misery, we got to see the steep decline we now had to take, and although going down may seem to be some form of relief, it was the sight of Agony up ahead that almost made us all cry. The second hill, Agony, would begin shortly after we were completely done with Misery, and its steep slope upward seemed worse than the one we had just completed.

The yelling and cursing of our drill sergeants took on a different message while hiking up Agony. As we agonized our way up the hill, drill sergeants would preach to us about pushing through the pain and making way for our heart, for it was our hearts that would help us push through just about anything. It really wasn't preaching though.

"I don't think you have heart, privates! I think all you shit bags left your hearts back on Misery! You all have not felt pain yet! Not the type of pain that leaves you with nothing else other than the thoughts of your pathetic lives! Push your way to the top, privates, and show us that you have a heart!" Once again, we did not understand the message being yelled out to us. All we knew was that these assholes were putting us through an agonizing obstacle, and the pain we were feeling didn't give way to even listen to their rambling and yelling. That is, until we reached the top of Agony.

I remember looking up toward the top of the hill and hoping to push through to the finish. Willing myself to take a few more steps and make it all the way up. *I can do it. I can do it. I know I can do it.* Then in one of those steps I took, I looked up ahead toward the top of Agony, and I noticed something strange.

I noticed that the privates wouldn't portray relief or a sense of accomplishment as they reached the hilltop. I wondered why. Even with all the pain I was feeling on my legs, my feet, and the exhaustion that was slowly eating away at my determination, I began to feel fear.

Why were my platoon buddies not showing any signs of relief on the hilltop? What was going on? What were they seeing?

My sense of confusion actually allowed me to push through by making me forget all the pain going through my body. My mind was now focused on the hilltop and discovering what everyone else was seeing.

"Just a few more steps, privates! You're almost there! Push through it, give me all you got!"

I was getting closer. Fifteen steps away. I could now hear my platoon buddies gasp and groan ahead of me. Those sounds were sounds of defeat and not of relief or triumph.

Ten steps away. What the hell was going on? What was making the members of my platoon drop their heads in defeat as they conquer this hilltop?

Five steps away. As I reached the top, I could feel my nervousness and excitement giving way through the aches and pains surrounding my body. I was yelling out within me, "I've made it, I reached the top!" Then, in an instant, all my aches and pains came back to me and slapped me in a way that I can only describe as running into a brick wall. I felt shock, pain, defeat, fear, exhaustion, and most of all, heartbreak.

Standing in the distance was one more hill that we had to push through, the famously known hill, Heartbreak. All I could do wasere drop my shoulders and cry out within me that this couldn't be. Not another hill, and it even looked worse than the one I just marched up. I felt the weight of my Kevlar helmet push down on my entire being as I dropped my own head in defeat.

Now I understood the rest of my platoon. Now I understood the rants and ramblings of my drill sergeants. This was where our young hearts were being tested. A hill true to its name.

Two days later, we were made to run all three hills, and our platoon dwindled some more. We must have done the Trinity Trail at least once every two weeks, and we all got better at it with time, but we still struggled with Heartbreak every single time. Our rucks were packed heavier every time we did the march, and the physical beating before our runs was made worse as well.

I think our drill sergeants wanted to make sure that the hills would always be a challenge and would always be feared. They were successful in that regard.

Graduating from basic training was bittersweet. I was happy and relieved that I had been successful in all our testing and was graduating from this grueling training. Yet all the happiness I was experiencing was also the reason of my sadness.

My entire family was still living just below the poverty line, and nobody could afford to make the trip and see me graduate. All I could do on the Sunday before graduating was call my mother and grandfather to let them know that I had made it through this first phase of training. They were happy for me and congratulated me over the pay phone. I wanted to see the look on their faces, I wanted to share this experience with them, and although I was proud of my accomplishment, I also felt all alone.

That lonesome feeling changed on the day of our dress rehearsal. All of us had to wear our dress uniforms so that we could be inspected by our drill sergeants and be given the approval of our first sergeant. I should say our commanding officer, but I don't remember seeing him that much throughout our training.

I remember all of us checking one another's uniform out prior to formation and helping one another out with minor things on our brass, our shoes, our ties, and coats. All of a sudden, Drill Sergeant Rios made his way into our barracks area and began talking to us like a normal person. This was somewhat shocking and made us feel uneasy.

He was telling us about having made it to the end of our training and how proud he was of us. "Men, let me be the first to tell you that you are no longer shit bags! You have become men, you have become soldiers. More importantly, you have become members of my brethren!"

I couldn't believe what I was hearing. Did he just call us brothers?

Then something unexpected happened. Drill Sergeant Rios faced me and walked toward me. The way he walked in his dress uniform was impressive; this man had been a part of Desert Storm and had apparently accomplished a lot throughout his career. I say this because his chest was very well decorated with campaign ribbons and medals that he had earned throughout his years of service.

Up until that moment, I had never been in the presence of a highly decorated soldier. I was literally stunned by what I was seeing and more so by what I was feeling. Something about seeing my own drill sergeant in dress uniform with all his accomplishments on display made me feel proud. This was unlike any sense of pride that I had had before. I was in shock. This man had been my leader for a period of two months, and now all I wanted to do was to somehow emulate him.

This sense of pride only grew stronger as Drill Sergeant Ruff walked in wearing his dress uniform. He too just stood there looking at all of us and, I daresay, admiring us. It was as if he were proud of the product he had created in us. It would be years before I could look at a group of individuals and have that same feeling of proud accomplishment.

A few minutes later, we were joined by Drill Sergeant Shep, our senior drill. He was definitely our senior drill sergeant for a reason; the medals on his uniform just about covered the entire left side of his chest. All three drill sergeants had combat patches on their right sleeve. All three were highly decorated while we, their privates, didn't have anything. Yet they all had the same look on their faces. They were proud of the soldiers they had made out of us.

I have never been able to forget that moment, for it was then and there that I wanted to become a leader. Not just a manager, a leader such as those men who had torn me down to nothing and then built me back up to become a soldier. A leader who didn't have to state his accomplishments, a leader who could show and prove that he deserved that title, that role, that respect.

After our graduation ceremony, Drill Sergeant Shep walked over to me and asked, "How do you feel, Private Tinoco?"

Private Tinoco? Had he just pronounced my name correctly? Had I moved up from being Private *Tinko*?

"I feel great, Drill Sergeant!"

Two days later, I was en route to Fort Lee, Virginia, for my Advanced Individual Training (AIT). The travel arrangements to Fort Lee were all done by the military, and since the location was only ten hours away driving, those of us going there were placed on a bus and transported to our new training location.

Fort Lee was not as bad as Fort Knox was; the physical demand we experienced during AIT was not as stringent. This is where I had to go in order to learn my actual job in the army.

My MOS was 92A, logistics specialist. That is way too fancy a title for someone working in a military vehicles parts store. That was my specialized job. I would dispatch vehicles when needed, order parts for vehicles when needed, and handle returns for parts that could be repaired, recycled, or refurbished. Nothing tactical about it when explained like this.

The thing about my job is that it was a support job. This meant that I could be assigned to any type of military unit since all units had military equipment, whether they be Abrams tanks, five tons, Humvees, or even helicopters. So I could be assigned to a medical unit, an infantry unit, an armor unit, and even a unit that contained the army's Special Forces element.

Whatever our assigned unit did, we did. Wherever our assigned unit went, we went. Soldiers that do the logistics job are pretty much embedded with their assigned units and get to partake in most of those units' tasks, whether it be in peace or war.

Probably the greatest lesson I learned at Fort Lee with regard to my job was that, if you took care of the different military elements you supported, they would almost always take care of you. I say *almost always* because it all depended on what I would ask for.

In most cases, whenever I heard the words "Tinoco, whatever you need or want, just say so," I would almost always ask the different platoon sergeants to allow me to partake in their specialized training or to take soldiers in my crew for patrols whenever they went. There were a few times in my military career that this was not feasible. Yet there were a few times when I ended up paying the price later on in life for having been granted what I asked for. Those times, I actually got involved in fights I had no business getting involved in and saw things that someone with my military specialty truly had no business seeing.

In essence, the gratitude of others placed me in situations that are normally not experienced by a 92A logistics specialist or supervisor.

HHC 2/5 CAV—Black Knights

. . . .

Headquarters and Headquarters Company, Second Battalion, Fifth Cavalry Regiment (HHC 2/5 CAV), was my first duty assignment. The unit is part of the First Cavalry Division and is located in Fort Hood, Texas. I arrived at the unit on the same day that my first-ever squad leader, Sergeant Bess, arrived. We both met as we were filling out some initial unit entry forms and as we were waiting on the sergeant major to meet with us.

The unit is a mechanized infantry unit and at that time was slated as a rapid deployment unit that was constantly conducting training events in various settings since it wasn't quite clear where the next deployment would be. With that in mind, the unit was to always remain trained and ready to deploy. The unit was mostly known for its Bradley Fighting Vehicles and their scouts. It had some of the meanest, toughest, and harshest leadership that I got to experience during my military career.

Sergeant Bess was a skinny, bow-legged tall black man who loved to run and loved to do his job. The man knew more about army logistics than I could have ever learned. His downside, of course, in my mind, was that he loved to run. I hated running, I hate running to this day. Ironic when you stop to consider the fact that I had to run all the time in the military and follow up with a career in chasing people after my time in service.

In any case, we met with the sergeant major, and he informed us of the unit's standards, demands, and requirements of the chain of command. He then informed us of a book titled *We Were Soldiers Once . . . and Young: Ia Drang—the Battle That Changed the War in Vietnam*, by retired lieutenant general Harold G. Moore and war journalist Joseph L.

Galloway. The book later became a movie, which starred Mel Gibson. The sergeant major basically told us to get the book, read it, and own up to the same core strengths, guts, and bravery as those depicted in the true story of that book. This was the first military book I had ever read.

On-the-job training was fairly simple when you eliminate all the yelling, cursing, and pranking that are commonplace in any military unit when you first arrive. The pranks were the best, and I am guilty of having played the same pranks on other soldiers as they first arrived in the unit after me.

My favorite one actually involved different departments within our unit and normally took all day long. This prank was normally done to get rid of a new soldier when he is being more of a nuisance than a helping hand. Hey, sometimes we just didn't have the time to actually explain everything to soldiers. This prank was also done on me when I first arrived. Please keep in mind, though, that I was clueless to most of these pranks and this way of life.

Since I worked in logistics, my actual workshop was located in the motor pool. This is the area in which all our military vehicles are kept. Here you will normally find all the unit's mechanics, fuel shop guys, and our communications soldiers. The motor pool at that time was about two miles away from the actual unit where all the administrative offices were, along with supply, infantry, scouts, medics, and mortar platoons.

The prank normally began in the morning around 0800 hours, after breakfast. Our squad leader would inform all the other soldiers in the squad about it so that everyone would be in on it. As soon as we all reported to the shop, Sergeant Bess instructed me to go to the supply office at the company area and get some grid squares from them. It is important to note that military maps are patterned with grid squares so that we may plot coordinates from said squares on a map and be able to make our way to a specified location. Once I left the motor pool, Sergeant Bess called the supply office and informed the supply sergeant of the prank being pulled. Remember, I am still a private at this time and am expected to still run everywhere, especially being a part of a mechanized infantry unit. So I ran over to the supply shop and reported to the sergeant as directed. Supply sergeant looked at me and asked what I needed. I stood there like the idiot private and stated my instructions of being there to pick up a box of grid squares.

The supply sergeant, in turn, handed me an old, worn map, a pair of scissors, and a small cardboard box.

I took the items and, still puzzled, asked, "Excuse me, Sergeant, but what am I supposed to do with this?"

"They asked you for grid squares, right?"

"Yes, Sergeant."

"Then I suggest you start cutting all those grid squares off the map and place them in the box I gave you. Oh, and make sure you cut them perfectly because that is the last set of grid squares that we have. You better not screw this up! Also, you have to do it here; I don't want you taking off with my scissors."

Being the good soldier, I cut up all the grid squares off the map and placed them inside the box. As I was about to leave, the supply sergeant stopped me and gave me other instructions as he handed me another box.

"Private Tinoco, before you leave, I need you to take these chemlight batteries over to Staff Sergeant Mandy in the motor pool and ask him for the status on my left-handed wrench while you're there."

"Yes, Sergeant!"

Well, it turns out that chemlights don't require any batteries and there is no such thing as a left-handed wrench. Yet being the squared-away soldier that I was or wanted to be, I followed my last order and drove on.

Another run and two miles later, I arrived at my shop and handed the box of grid squares to Sergeant Bess. He opened the box, and all hell broke loose.

"What the hell is this, Tinoco?"

"Do you know what you've done, Private? Holy shit, son!"

Sergeant Bess threw the cardboard box across the shop and continued yelling as everyone else in my squad just listened. Me, I was terrified. What the hell did I do?

"Can you all believe this shit? Do you all see what the hell this private just did? How the fuck are we ever going to win a war like this? Where the hell are you from, Private?"

Stuttering, I said, "I'm from the Rio Grande Valley, Sergeant."

"Rio Grande what? They might as well call that shit hole, Rio Grande Dumb Ass! Who the hell is supposed to be teaching you the ropes around here, Private?"

Unsure and scared shitless, I answered, "I, I, I'm not sure, Sergeant. You haven't told me."

"Holy shit! So now you're telling me I am not doing my job! Are you all listening to this bullshit?"

Now I was starting to panic. "No, Sergeant!"

"Then what the fuck are you saying, Private? Do you not know English?"

"Yes, Sergeant!"

"Yes, I'm not doing my job, or yes, you speak fucking English, because it sure as hell doesn't sound like English to me! You know what, forget it! I don't have time for this shit. Were you instructed to do anything else by the supply sergeant?"

"Yes, Sergeant."

"Then get the hell out of my face and go do it!"

I don't think I knew which way to run. I couldn't get out of there fast enough. In my panic, I saw someone walking into our shop, and I just ran straight for the door. Luckily, I didn't forget the chemlight batteries in my frantic state.

For the life of me, I couldn't understand what I had done wrong. I followed my instructions word for word.

I made it over to Staff Sergeant Mandy's shop and handed him the box of batteries.

He just sat there, mean old man who actually looked like Hitler on steroids with his shitty little mustache. He looked into the box, actually smiled, looked up at me, and asked, "What are these?"

"Supply Sergeant said you needed chemlight batteries, Staff Sergeant!" His smile grew even more now.

"And let me guess, he also wants to know the status on his left-handed wrench."

"Yes, Staff Sergeant!"

"No need to sound off, Private . . . Tikono, Teeneeko—which is it, Private?"

Oh, hell no. I'm not falling for that shit again in correcting a sergeant on the pronunciation of my name. I've learned my lesson.

"You pronounced it just right, Staff Sergeant!"

"I think you're full of shit there, Teeneeko, but I give less than a rat's ass about your fucking name."

In my mind, I was thinking, *Well, I don't care that you don't care, as long as you don't smoke my ass for correcting you on the pronunciation of my name.*

He pulled open a drawer of his desk and pulled out a wrench. "Look at this wrench. Do you see anything special about it?"

"No, Staff Sergeant."

"Well, here is your first motor-pool lesson, Tikono. There is no such thing as a left-handed wrench. Someone is fucking with you. Just go back to your squad leader, Sergeant Bess, and I'll talk to the supply sergeant."

"Yes, Staff Sergeant."

What the hell was going on? As I walked back to my shop—I wasn't running again. Fuck that; things began to click somehow in my mind. I mean, I knew what chemlights were—hell, we used them at basic training. I might not have been mechanically inclined, but I knew better than to believe there was such a thing as a left-handed wrench. Shit, they got me. All that was left was the whole matter of the grid squares with Sergeant Bess.

I must have had a strange, bewildered look on my face when I walked into the shop because everyone busted out laughing the moment I walked in. Sergeant Bess walked over to me and smacked me on the back. "Tinoco, do you realize that you just cut up a perfectly good military map for no damn reason?"

Everyone was still laughing, assholes.

"Now I do, Sergeant. That was messed up, funny, but messed up." I started laughing as well.

It was a good one, and I can't even remember how many times I used it on other soldiers as the years went by. That shit never got old.

Our shop was pretty diverse. Sergeant Bess was our squad leader. We had two other sergeants in the shop. Sergeant Mack was white, and Sergeant Sep was Puerto Rican. Our squad of soldiers was comprised of three Mexicans, a white guy, and a red-headed black guy named Jack.

Jack was the one who truly took me under his wing and showed me the ropes, not only of the army, Fort Hood, the unit, but also on many things about life. My guess is that Jack had taken a lot of crap throughout his lifetime for being a red-headed black man that he pretty much knew how to best counter a lot of the shit that came our way at work and off work.

The other two Mexicans in our shop were actually from New Braunfels, Texas, and they were already third- or fourth-generation bona fide American citizens. Not simpleton Mexicans like me. They were actually cousins. What were the odds of that? Two cousins from the same town ending up in the same army unit at Fort Hood, Texas. They weren't that far away from home at all, the duo of Mike and John.

Mike was the younger of the two and the craziest one. John was older and more mature. Yet it seemed at that time that they had both lived far, distant lives from mine, and it caused a couple of clashes between us from time to time. Either way, they were good guys, and they did their best to teach me all they could about being a Hispanic in Central Texas.

George, was our token white guy, aside from Sergeant Mack. I can best describe George as your typical Joe Dirt in an army uniform. He was funny as hell and meant well but could never somehow piece the puzzle together on anything we ever did. This made our jobs that much more fun yet caused our work to take longer as well.

Our job was simple: dispatch vehicles and equipment to the soldiers for daily operations, training events, and even deployments. Without the automated dispatch, a piece of equipment could not be operated. We worked together with the mechanics in the motor pool because they would let us know if a vehicle or piece of equipment was operable or not.

Whenever maintenance was performed on the equipment, mechanics would come to us so that we could order any parts they needed for said equipment. We did keep some automotive parts in stock at the shop, and each one of us was assigned to a particular company of the battalion. Some of the parts we stocked or that the vehicles needed would be items that could be turned back into the army for refurbishing, while others were simply turned back into the system for recycling purposes.

Since our unit was a mechanized infantry unit whose main fighting power was that of Bradly Fighting Vehicles, we dealt with many heavy and expensive automotive parts. Lugging some of those road wheels and tractor shoes for the tracked vehicles was not an easy thing to do. For much of the stuff, we had to utilize a forklift to load or unload the parts from our assigned deuces, M35, two-and-a-half-ton cargo trucks.

They were more commonly known as deuce and a half, and they were beasts. They could go through just about any training terrain we ever encountered. The ride itself was rough as hell, and most of us had no mercy whatsoever on our passenger whenever we had one, especially when we were out in the field.

I remember so many times when my own passenger would be dozing off from the exhaustion and the constant rumbling sound of the truck. It was during those moments that I would normally ram the truck toward a BFH or BFR; those are big fucking holes or big fucking rocks.

The site of the passenger's head slamming against the door window or top portion of the metal frame was always funny as hell. The best ones would be when we were forced to wear our helmets while operating the vehicle. That big old thing weighing heavily on our heads and then slamming against the window was always good for a laugh.

Many of my passengers would actually try to play it off and act as if they had not been falling asleep. When they did that, I looked for even-bigger fucking holes and bigger fucking rocks. Fun times, fun times indeed.

The great thing about our shop and the military in general was that we were a pretty diverse group of men. This meant that we could talk trash to one another on any subject and for any freaking reason. We truly had some colorful conversations. The other great thing about being assigned to that unit was that we could talk however the hell we wanted to talk since there were no women assigned to the unit.

If we weren't talking trash or constantly swearing to one another, something was wrong. Just don't let someone else from outside the unit talk trash to you, because then all hell would break loose. It was funny when you think about it. We could tear one another down because we were all in the same unit, but we could never allow for a soldier from another unit talk trash to any of us, because a fight would ensue.

Our own sergeant major told us all in formation one Friday morning, "Men, do not let me hear that soldiers from the Black Knights Regiment leave behind one of their fellow soldiers behind at some bar to get a beating.

"If this happens, I will personally come over to your barracks and commence to whoop some ass.

"If there are more of them, I expect a phone call, and I will send the entire battalion to that fucking bar and make sure that the Black Knights win the fight!

"Do I make myself clear?"

In roaring thunder, we answered, "Roger that, Sergeant Major!"

"Now, if cops get to the bar and break the fight up, someone better call me so that I can go straighten out the mess.

"None of my men, and I do mean *none of my* men, will be hauled over to some local jailhouse for helping out their fellow soldiers without my expressed permission!

"Am I understood?"

Again in roaring, thunderous military fashion, we answered, "Yes, Sergeant Major!"

That was all it took. Those were our weekly instructions, and for the most part, the leadership of the Black Knights lived up to this statement. Now this didn't mean that a soldier was not going to get punished for his actions; it just meant that the soldier or soldiers would receive in-house punishment and not have to deal with actual civilian charges, which might hinder the soldiers' careers.

It must have been about six months after I arrived at Fort Hood that I began drinking and getting into stupid shit with the rest of the soldiers around me. I may be stretching that out a bit though.

One night, I went out to a local bar with a few friends. We were all just having a good time drinking and playing pool. I wasn't drinking, because I was not twenty-one yet. This also meant that I was the designated driver during all our outings.

To my friends, I was Junior. I was Junior for several reasons. One, I was the youngest in the group. Two, I was the newest addition to our platoon. Three and probably most important, I was barely beginning to learn about life. I had spent my entire childhood and adolescent years working without learning much about getting stupid with friends and just doing crazy things. This pretty much meant I was everyone's pupil, and oh, what a dangerous situation that was.

Well, a few of us were at the local bar, playing pool, listening to some country music, and all my buddies were having some beer. As in any bar with pool tables, someone eventually ended up bumping into someone else or someone accused another person of messing up their shot.

It just so happened that, on that particular night, Eddie, one of my friends, accidentally bumped into a player on the pool table next to ours. This, in turn, supposedly messed up that guy's professional shot of the evening. The fun began.

Eddie immediately turned over toward the "professional pool player" and actually apologized for having bumped into him.

The pro said, "What the fuck, man, you messed up my shot, asshole!"

"My bad, bro. I'm sorry, I didn't mean to."

"The hell you didn't mean to, you piece of shit!"

Being the sober one in the group, I quickly made my way over to Eddie and started trying to end the entire situation before it got out of hand. I even offered to get the professional and his buddies a pitcher of beer.

One problem though, I couldn't buy beer for being underage, and my group of guys was not backing me up on the gesture.

"Fuck that shit, Junior! Eddie already apologized, man; that should be enough! This fucktard is being a prima donna, acting like we messed up a professional shot or something!"

By this time, both groups were closing in on me, Eddie, and the professional, and everyone was now starting to get loud.

I somehow managed to raise my voice louder than anyone's and ask them all to just chill out, relax, and enjoy the rest of the night. "Come on, guys, nothing happened here. Let's just all get some drinks and just relax."

I forgot to mention that the professional was taller than me by about six or seven inches and I was just about that much taller than Eddie. Apparently, that gave him the floor whenever he chose to speak. How could he not think that way? He was a tall white country boy inside a country bar, and some Mexican had just messed up his shot.

"Junior? That's what your boys call you? You're just a piece of shit spic to me!"

Out of nowhere, I saw fists flying around me toward the professional. "Oh, hell no! Nobody talks shit to Junior but us!"

And just like that, all hell broke loose.

At the end of it all, four pool tables were broken, a bunch of cue sticks were broken in half, pool balls were all over the bar, and most of us had bloody noses, along with a few banged-up hands, and all our clothes were disheveled. A bunch of red and blue lights were lighting up the sky outside the bar as police officers were interviewing the bartenders and a few of the witnesses not involved in the fight.

Then out of nowhere, this huge lifted pickup truck arrived at the parking lot, and our sergeant major stepped down from the driver's side. One of the bartenders actually walked over toward the sergeant major and began to explain the entire ordeal as he pointed at us and then at the professional's group of soldiers.

I began to shit bricks. I mean, the cops were here, the bar was a mess, we were all torn up, along with the other group, and now our sergeant major was here.

I watched the sergeant major like a hawk as he made his way toward the police officers and began to chat with them. He looked over at us, looked inside the bar, and then scanned over the other soldiers as though assessing the damage done to them and comparing it to the damage we endured.

After a few minutes of conversing with the cops, he walked over to us.

"Men! The bartender has filled me in on all the details. It seems that you all actually tried to squash this whole mess before it even began. I like that. Hell, I like that a lot."

He looked over toward the other soldiers. "What I like the most of this whole ordeal is that those soldiers over there look a hell of a lot more fucked up than you all do.

"You all make the Black Knights proud."

He eyed us all as he took a long sigh. "Now get your shit, and get your fucking asses onto my truck!"

I don't think any of us hesitated. We all just ran and limped toward the back of his pickup truck and jumped into it. None of us were saying a word, and I don't think any of us said a damn thing the entire way back to our barracks.

Once we got to our barracks, the sergeant major told us all to hit the sack and to figure out how to get our vehicles the next day from the bar.

"Don't leave your vehicles there, because they will be towed and you'll have to spend more of your beer money for that shit."

That was the extent of it all. None of us got into any serious trouble over the incident. We did catch a lot of crap the following Monday morning at formation and during our PT session, but nothing serious at all. We did receive a warning per se that indicated that one event was our freebie. Any other events would be dealt with accordingly by our chain of command.

I was stationed at Fort Hood, Texas, for a total of six years. In those six years, I think we went to the National Training Center in Fort Irwin, California, every single year. Sometimes we would go in the summertime, which was horrible since the training center is within the Mojave Desert. Other times, we would go in the wintertime, which was just as horrible because of the drastic changes in temperature that took place at dusk and dawn.

The training itself was only four weeks long, but it was a horrible four weeks for my shop. Being that we were the ones in charge of dispatching all operational equipment, we had to first input all that equipment and then the assigned operators into our computer systems.

All the other elements of our unit only had to worry about their assigned vehicles and equipment. We had to worry about everyone's vehicles when they were drawn out for training and when they were turned back in to Fort Irwin after the training was over. Talk about having some sleepless nights and even worse days.

Every battalion and its assigned companies had designated sleeping areas during the initial week for drawing out equipment and during the last week for turning-in said equipment. The soldiers in my shop slept wherever we crashed.

We would collapse outside our work tent, on top of our duffel bags, most of the time, and if we wanted to get an extra hour of shut-eye, we would find a vehicle that was already turned in and collapse inside it.

Sleep was a precious commodity that we didn't have much of during training events.

A quartermaster's job is 24-7. Other platoons get to do training whenever the entire unit is not actually training, while quartermasters such as myself and those in my shop actually have work to do whether we are training, deployed, or back at garrison. We work hand in hand with those in maintenance and have to deal with so many different professions within the military service. Medics, supply personnel, cooks, infantrymen, scouts, mortarmen, etc.

We are one of the few professions that soldiers know all too well not to mess with. Soldiers do not mess with cooks, or their food will be jacked up one way or another or their field rations may not be as adequate as one would wish.

They don't mess with supply personnel, for they are the ones who get the soldiers all their needed supplies for actual work, training, and deployment. Go ahead and run out of batteries or other field essentials, and see whom you go running to.

The Automated Logistics Shop, or the PLL (Prescribed Load List) Dispatch shop, as soldiers often referred to us, is another shop not to be messed with. A soldier's vehicle or operations equipment is his or her lifeline in the field and at garrison. It must be taken care of in order to remain in the game.

Go ahead and piss off a soldier working in my shop. I guarantee that the parts you need for your vehicle to remain operational will somehow take a long time to get to the maintenance guys. Oh, and those returnable items that can be refurbished and must be turned in to us for proper disposition, that stuff is going to get kicked back for dumb shit several times at least. Just to prove a point.

"Don't fuck with the quartermasters." Quartermasters have the power to leave a soldier out of the game completely if pushed the wrong way. It's important to remember that, regardless of the task at hand, soldiers always have something else to do or something better to do in their minds, and they don't like to be held back.

This was the relationship that I exploited throughout my military career. The fact that our shop was an integral part of any unit's or platoon's operational readiness came in handy whenever I wanted to learn something new. Most times, I just wanted to be allowed to train with the "cool" guys doing all the cool stuff, like learning field patrol techniques, shooting new weapons, blowing shit up, and even something as simple as learning to drive the various pieces of equipment we had in our unit.

It was these "favors" that ultimately ended up becoming the reasons behind my nightmares today. It was because of the various things I learned from these different platoons that I was able to do and see things that many quartermasters don't ever get to experience throughout their careers, but I'm getting ahead of myself here and will get to those particulars later on.

In my remembering of hairy moments at the National Training Center, one night comes to mind.

Throughout our training events at NTC, there are various live-fire exercises that the units are put through. Sometimes the actual notification of exact locations where live rounds are going to be shot at comes a bit late, as was the case one cold night.

Being the PLL Shop entails that half of us are always near the front lines along with most of our unit and their respective maintenance crew. This is done so that we can be on hand with any necessary parts should a piece of equipment take fire and be temporarily decommissioned from the fight. This is only for those fighting vehicles that can be fixed quickly and thrown back into the mix.

The other half of our shop remains farther back with the main support element to handle all other situations and vehicles that cannot be fixed quickly and actually need far more than just a few parts from us. This portion of our shop also pushes forward whatever line items are being exhausted near the front lines in order to keep our fighting forces engaged as much as possible.

On this particular night, my buddy Jack and I were part of the front element, and it was in the middle of the night after we had already decided to get some sleep. All of a sudden, Staff Sergeant Mandy came over to our vehicles since we would be operational from them in the "front" and told us to shut everything down and get ready to move out.

"Tinoco! Break all your shit down and get ready to move. They're about to start a live-fire exercise, and we are sitting in the target zone!"

I jumped straight out of my sleeping bag. "Holy shit, Sarge, is this shit for real?"

"Yes, goddamit! Now move your ass and let your partners know we are moving out in ten mikes!"

I was already putting on my boots and jumping off my deuce and a half by the time he finished rattling that crap. My first stop was to Jack's vehicle.

"Jack! Jack!" I shouted as I was climbing onto the back of his deuce. "Jack! Wake the hell on up, we got to go, man!"

"What the fuck, Tinoco?"

"Dude, get the fuck up! SSG Mandy said we are rolling out in ten because we are about to get shot at for some stupid live-fire exercise!"

"Are you shitting me? Of all the fucking things, holy shit, Tinoco!" I was already running away to John's truck to let him know the same thing, and some of our battalion support element had been camping out at our site as well due to some heavy lifting that had to be done. Those guys had been gracious enough to bring their forklift with them, and now they were about to get shot the hell up.

Our temporary staging area was all woken up, alert, and moving equipment everywhere within moments while SSG Mandy and our warrant officer, Chief Pike, kept on yelling at everyone to move quicker and start lining up behind the chief's vehicle since he would be leading our convoy to safety.

The entire ordeal was chaotic, engines revving up, soldiers cursing, griping, and we still had to practice light discipline, of all freaking things.

Light discipline! Can you believe that shit!

This meant we could not have any lights on at all while we were getting ready to move out or during the movement itself. Lucky for us, we had some moonlight to help us out, but our maintenance guys were sucking because they had to tow whatever piece of equipment was being worked on.

Latching those vehicles onto our tow trucks and tanks was not an easy task in the cover of darkness and with our lives on the line, to top shit off. Chemlights were flying everywhere as we all worked together to try to get everyone ready to go.

Jack and John made sure I had all my gear and was ready to go since I was the lowest-ranking soldier of the squad at that time. Those guys always took care of me, especially Jack.

"Tinoco, you ready, man?" he said as he checked my frag vest, weapon, night-vision goggles (NVGs). "Yeah, bro. I'm good to go, man."

"Okay, here's our lineup. John will be in the front, you in the middle, and I'll be behind you. The battalion support element will be behind me with their rig since they're pulling that fucking forklift."

"Okay, okay, I got it."

"Get in your deuce, and don't fall behind, because we are driving dark, no lights, so keep your NVGs on and don't lose sight of John's deuce!"

We all got into our vehicles as Staff Sergeant Mandy and Chief began to yell out that we were moving out. I was nervous; the thought of being shot at during training by mortars and other shit was not a good feeling at all.

The convoy began rolling out, and as one would expect in the desert, dust began to fly all over the place. This only worsened as we were truly driving hard and fast out of the area. I could barely see the cat eyes of John's deuce in front of me because of all the sand flying everywhere. Luckily, with time, my eyes adjusted to the situation, and I could follow John without any problems.

There were moments throughout that drive that I had to haul ass because the convoy kept speeding up. The vehicles were all bouncing as we hit rocks and holes on the ground and continued to move forward as fast as we could and as careful as we possibly could. Speed was the priority, though.

With all the bouncing around during the drive, it was difficult to keep my NVGs directly in front of me. They were mounted on my Kevlar but kept on shifting with every jolt the vehicle made. It was in one of those moments that I was adjusting them in place for me to see better that I saw John's night-vision taillights brighten up and stay lit. I quickly slammed on my own brakes and the other vehicles behind me followed suit. I heard Jack right away.

"What the fuck, Tinoco? Why are we stopping?"

I simply reacted, immediately jumped out of my truck, and ran toward John's.

"John! John! Are you okay, man?"

"No, bro, I hit a big fucking rock and blew my front tire. I can't fucking keep going! Can't believe this shit!"

I quickly ran toward Jack as he was making his way to us. "Jack, let's get that fucking forklift down fast! John's rig has a busted tire, man!"

"You got to be shitting me, Tinoco!" Then he must have seen the expression on my face or my seriousness in the darkness because, the moment he looked at me, he began running toward the battalion support element with me.

"Hey, get that forklift down, man, we got a busted tire on a deuce, and we need to lift that shit fast before we get blown to pieces!"

Just as we were coordinating the forklift situation, Staff Sergeant Mandy drove up on our location, kicking sand everywhere with his Humvee, demanding to know why the hell we had stopped the convoy.

Jack explained the situation to him as I continued to help getting the forklift down from the flatbed it was on and escort the driver over to John's deuce.

Staff Sergeant Mandy jumped off his vehicle and ran toward John to help him get the spare tire off the truck. John was already underneath the rear of his truck, messing with the spare.

All of us were walking with chemlights in our hands and in our mouths due to the light discipline, even in this shitty situation. Rules are rules. Jack and I quickly guided the forklift to the front of the deuce and used our chemlights to light up the deuce's front bumper for the forklift operator to see. Forks were slid underneath the bumper, and the deuce was lifted high enough off the sand for us to work on replacing the tire.

We worked like a NASCAR team on that tire. The busted one was off and the replacement was on in a matter of seconds. We were men on a mission, and nothing was stopping us. Jack and I hauled the bad tire behind the deuce and just threw that thing onto the trailer that John was pulling. That trailer was full of road wheels and track shoes for our Bradley Fighting Vehicles and some of our Medic Tracks.

We then guided the forklift back toward the flatbed and helped the operator secure it prior to heading back toward John and Staff Sergeant Mandy.

"All good, Sarge!"

"All right, guys, we have split from the main convoy, so now I'll be the lead, and you all try to keep up! We gotta get the fuck out of dodge, so keep up and watch out for those big fucking rocks!"

Staff Sergeant Mandy took the lead of our group and was able to drive us out of the impact area onto a safety zone where Chief Pike was already waiting on us with the rest of the convoy.

I don't think any of us got any sleep until the following night once we had settled down at another location and began our normal operations again for the training event.

It was moments like this that always brought us closer together. Here we were again, on the verge of being blown to pieces during a training event, and we somehow always came together as one to get things done. That is the military life. Rank, nationalities, backgrounds, religions, age differences, and mind-sets all set aside for the common goal of helping your brethren. Awesome stuff.

The rest of that particular training cycle went without incident as our days and nights continued with little rest and far less sleep. We couldn't wait to get back to Fort Hood.

Military Deployment

· · · · · · · · · · · · · · · · · · ·

Probably the toughest thing about military deployments that people don't discuss is the fact that soldiers, after having been gone so long, feel completely out of place in their own homes.

While being deployed to other countries in order to fight whatever war is currently being fought, life continues at home without the soldier. All the tasks that may seem mediocre and are more than likely taken for granted by most, such as cutting the lawn, taking out trash, fixing things inside the house, and even the task of picking up one's kids from school are left behind to be done by someone else in the family.

Most of the times, it is the wife or the husband, depending on who stayed behind that ends up picking up the tab on all those tasks. It is basic human behavior; those things must still be done, and in time, they become the responsibility of someone else other than the deployed soldier.

To make matters more complicated, everyone who was left behind continues to evolve as human beings. Trends change within the family circle. Our kids develop new habits, learn about new things, and they continue to grow and develop their own personalities without the presence of the soldier.

All these things are missed by the soldier during a military deployment. The soldier does not get to experience his or her kids' personalities begin to develop whether that be for the better or for the worse.

A soldier comes back from deployment expecting and wishing that everything is still the same. For the most part, things are the same. It's just that the family has learned to manage everything at home without the presence and, more importantly, without the need of the soldier.

So where does that leave us?

Our mind-sets are still in the past, and we now have to play catch-up with little time to do so. Catch-up on how much our kids have grown and changed. Catch-up on how our spouse has managed the household without us and in his or her own different way of doing things.

A soldier must now learn how to blend in and mingle with the new ways that the family is functioning. A soldier cannot assert his or her own will and judgment of things on day one. We have to accept immediately that we have been gone for so long and that things at home have changed. We must slowly embed ourselves again within our own homes and within our own families.

These things are not easy to deal with when we come back.

At least for me and the soldiers I deployed with, these things were not easy to deal with at all. Especially adding the fact that we still needed to decompress from our own way of life during the military deployment.

The only time a soldier has to decompress and set aside the feeling of being in a "hot zone" or in combat is the time it takes for the plane to get us home.

With that said, my first military deployment was to Bosnia and Herzegovina. I was on the plane to Bosnia on August 24, 1998, and when I arrived, there was a Red Cross message waiting for me from back home.

My first son was born while I was in flight. My first hour in the country, and I already felt and knew that I had lost so much. The realization of how much I had already missed and how much more I was about to miss with regard to my son was overwhelming. I was escorted by my battalion major over to a small shack and guided over to a phone that I could use to call the hospital.

We had just landed, the major looked at me, patted me on the back, congratulated me, and said, "You have five minutes, then we must leave."

My phone call was connected to the hospital where my son was born, and I was able to talk to his mother for a few minutes. I asked if the baby was okay and if everything had gone well during delivery. She and I were already at odds before my deployment, and although I had asked for my son to be named after the famous Mexican singer Marco Antonio Solís, she went with a slightly different version of the name instead.

When I asked why the change in name, I got an unexpected answer. She didn't want our son to have a name that could be seen or considered as being "too Mexican," and she had also decided to drop the *o* from his middle name. My middle name is Alberto, and she used Albert for my son.

Having just landed in Bosnia, I didn't want to start my deployment with an argument and decided to cut the call even shorter than five minutes. As I walked back outside to link up with my unit again, only one thought kept running through my mind: I didn't think I would be returning home to a family.

To make matters worse, I didn't know how long I would be in Bosnia. In our deployment briefings, we were constantly told that our deployment was only scheduled for six months but that it could last a year.

Having just arrived in the country, we were in the dark with regard to accurate timelines. A soldier sacrifices so much in order to accomplish a mission. My son's birth was my first lesson on this matter. Our unit deployed to Bosnia after their civil war from 1992 to 1995 had ended. There were a lot of people who still wanted us and the other NATO forces to leave so that they could continue to kill one another. We were supposed to be there as a peacekeeping force and to help them out with their first-ever democratic elections.

One of the most dangerous missions that the First Cavalry Division had throughout this deployment was the demining operation. Bosnia was known at that time to have over one million mines emplaced during its three-year civil war. Our engineers were placed in charge of the removal, dismantling, and the destruction of all land mines that could be found. This, of course, was to be done with the help and support of the entire First Cavalry Division and other NATO forces.

My battalion, the 2-5 Cavalry Regiment, was separated among different camps in country. Alpha Company was stationed in Camp McGovern, the most northern camp in country. They were near the borders of Croatia and Serbia. After leaving Camp Eagle in Tuzla, Bosnia, I never saw my coworker from the shop who handled all matters for Alpha Company until we were all back in Fort Hood, Texas.

Our Charlie Company clerk was stationed in Camp Comanche. We had to support our main Headquarters Company by way of a split operation. The support element of the company was positioned in Camp Dobol. Both Camp Comanche and Dobol were just a few hours south of Tuzla, with Camp Dobol being the nearest to the Serbian border.

I was sent to Camp Demi, along with another soldier in my squad. We would run our logistics operations for Bravo Company and the operational element of Headquarters Company. Camp Demi was the farthest south in country; it was located about four hours northeast of the city of Sarajevo.

None of us would see each other again until our deployment ended and we were all back at Fort Hood. Traveling toward Camp Demi was somewhat surreal. In seeing the ravaged remains of the country, you couldn't help but wonder if any peacekeeping mission could even succeed. This thought was more prevalent in Sarajevo.

Sarajevo is the capital of Bosnia and Herzegovina, and it was the host of the 1984 Winter Olympics, but you wouldn't be able to guess that as you drove through the city ruins during my time there. Their civil war had been so horrible and unpredictable that people couldn't even bury their dead in proper cemeteries.

I remember going on patrol with a few scouts of Headquarters Company and seeing crosses on burials on any patch of grass or dirt that was near apartment buildings, houses, shacks, and even businesses. It was shocking to think and realize that these people couldn't venture outside a building or structure too long because they were being killed by their opposing party the moment they stepped outside.

During one of our patrols, we had ventured off to see some of the old structures from the Winter Olympics and were not surprised to find them in ruin, riddled with evidence of their use as support structures during some intense fighting. The structures were covered with damage from bullets and explosions. The city and its surroundings were completely torn apart during the war.

Probably one of the more dangerous patrols that I was able to be a part of took us through the airport in Sarajevo. That place was completely destroyed. We could see planes still on the runway blown up and charred with blackness from all the fires that were surely caused by mortars and heavy artillery during their conflict.

Shortly after having passed by the airport, we began to take fire from the buildings around us. Our rules of engagement back then were very clear: we must have visual and 100 percent confirmation of an enemy combatant before we could open fire on any threat. All we could do was haul ass out of the area and continue to take gunfire as we made our way out of that spot.

I was a passenger on one of the Humvees, and even though we were all locked and loaded, we couldn't do anything. Our gunners sticking out of the Humvees were in a more precarious situation as they had to remain out there in search of targets as the gunfire continued. I had experienced fear before, but not a fear of such helplessness as this, listening to the bullets hit our armored vehicles as we sped off continually searching for a target. Our gunner wanted to shoot back; hell, we all did.

I remember the first lieutenant in charge of the patrol commanding us over the radio, asking for someone to get visual of a target, "Does anyone have visual of a target? Can anyone see clearly where the gunfire is coming from?"

None of us could; my eyes kept scanning frantically through every building that we passed as I'm sure all the scouts in our patrol were doing the same. We knew what we had to look for; we were all looking for a muzzle flash, but the gunfire we were taking was well coordinated. It wasn't long bursts of firing at all; it was simply single shots being fired at us.

A voice came out over the radio. "Sir, we have a general area of possible targets only, no visual confirmation! If we can't shoot back, then let's get the hell out of here!"

Just as that was called out, our gunner yelled out that he had visual. We were coming up on a blown-up old warehouse, and our gunner indicated that he had visual of four or five combatants firing at us. We called out the information over the radio as we still needed the lieutenant's green light.

"Okay, boys, light that shit up, light it all up!"

Our gunners all opened fire as we continued to speed through the street. Two of our Humvees had .50 -caliber machine guns on them, and the other two had MK19 automatic grenade launchers mounted on them.

After a few strings of fire, the pinging and zinging caused by the gunfire that was hitting our vehicles stopped momentarily only to help us confirm that we did have the right targets. Our Humvee stopped about a block away from the warehouse, and we all got out as quickly as possible and reached for cover on one of the buildings near the vehicle. Gunners remained on the Humvees.

We waited a few seconds. No shots.

The scouts all began their hand-signaling for movement toward the warehouse, and I followed suit. We made our way into the building with no further action taking place. We still had to reach the top floor, what was left of it, at least. Going through rubble from the civil war and the one we had just caused ourselves was a bit troublesome, yet we needed to confirm our kill for the reporting that was going to take place after this incident. Once we reached the top floor, a total of seven bodies was found, along with a stash of assorted weapons near them.

Once we all cleared the entire building and ensured there were no other combatants inside, the lieutenant called it in. We remained there for several hours until other brass showed up to take the lieutenant's report and begin to clear up the incident with the local officials.

My platoon sergeant and warrant officer were not pleased at all that I had been involved in this. I was not a scout or an infantryman. My job for this deployment was logistics, and that was done from within the "safety" of the camp I was in, not out on patrol. In the end, though, there wasn't much they could say since they had approved for me to ride along. It was a few months before I went out on patrol again.

Life inside Camp Demi, Bosnia, was pretty nice for a deployment. The camp was well made with small living quarters made out of what I can only describe as miniature mobile homes. They were about eight by fifteen feet in size, and all were made for two soldiers to share as a sleeping area.

There was a cafeteria, a gym, a barbershop that was operated by locals, and an entertainment area for watching movies, reading, and even attending online classes. Camp Demi also had a separate showering and restroom area that was located away from the sleeping quarters. There is nothing like going to the shower with full combat gear, "full battle rattle." Heck, we could never be out on the open anywhere in the camp without being fully geared up.

If I remember correctly, the camp had a total of eight guard towers, which needed to be manned 24-7. Each guard tower contained an automatic .50-caliber weapon on it and was manned by two soldiers at a time who also had their own M16s. There were also several bunkers throughout the camp should we ever need to take cover from mortars or other artillery.

Our work areas were completely separate from the common areas, and although our offices were also built out of the same miniature mobile home structures, the maintenance bays were not. Our mechanics had to work out of huge carport-type structures, which didn't offer much protection should we ever take fire from the outside.

The scary thing about Camp Demi was its actual location. It was at the bottom of a valley, surrounded by mountains. Just imagine a football field with the camp being on the field itself while the mountains and villages surrounding us made up the bleachers around that field. We would be the perfect target.

Christmas Eve of 1998, we were the perfect target.

For the most part, the guard towers were always being manned by every soldier on the camp. There were a few times that some platoons could not help on the guard towers because of operations, but we all shared the duty—scouts, infantrymen, mechanics, logistics clerks, cooks, and even medics.

Christmas Eve of 1998, I was stuck on guard duty at one of the towers. It was freezing outside, and the entire ground was covered in snow because we had just been through a blizzard a few nights before. Aside from the soldiers on the guard towers, we also had four soldiers patrolling on the ground along the fence. They would rotate with the soldiers on the towers from time to time in an attempt at staying somewhat warm throughout the day and night.

As soldiers, we did what we always do during holidays on a deployment. We discussed all things "back home" and told one another how our families celebrated the holiday and what we would be doing at that particular moment. Holidays are tough when you're away from those you love and care for, so we make the best with what we have and reminisce about times passed.

This particular Christmas Eve, though, our conversations were cut short.

It was just past midnight, already Christmas Day, when my partner noticed something peculiar on my chest.

"Tinoco, get the fuck down!" he yelled as he grabbed me by the frag vest and slammed me onto the floor.

"What the hell are you doing, man? What the fuck did you do that for?"

My partner didn't have time to answer at all before the radio on our tower began to broadcast. All our towers had a communications radio that was directly connected to the sergeant of the guard's (SOG) shack in the center of the camp. I went to grab for the receiver and froze.

I looked over to my partner and realized he was already looking at me as well; the entire inner wall of our tower was lit up with small red dots. The SOG kept on calling for Tower Three.

"Man, we have to get this. The SOG may have news about this shit," I told the other soldier.

"Tinoco, we are being targeted. Do you fucking realize that?"

"Yes!"

I quickly grabbed the receiver. "Tower Three, Specialist Tinoco here."

"Specialist Tinoco, this is SSG Miller, the SOG. Are you being targeted?"

"Yes, Sarge."

"I need you to man the .50 cal and have your partner scan with his 16. Do you copy?"

"Sarge, we are being targeted. Can we fire in the direction those pings are coming from?"

"No!" I said again.

"No! Under no circumstance will you fire your weapons! All our towers are being targeted, and we can't shoot unless we have visual confirmation of an actual combatant. You know this already, Specialist!"

"Sarge, how the hell do you want us to just stand here?"

"Do as you're told! The scouts have been alerted to our situation and are gearing up to roll out of the wire. You are not to fire until given the okay to do so. Do you understand!"

"I copy, Sarge."

I hung up the receiver and hesitated as I looked at my partner. "You heard the man, we have to man the gun, and we can't shoot at anything until we are given the okay."

"That's insane!"

"I know, Miles, but we have to. Come on." I made my way up toward the .50 cal and helped Miles up off the floor.

We couldn't stop staring at all the red dots surrounding our heads and chests. We locked and loaded, and terrified we began to scan the darkness outside the wire.

Once again, no visible targets.

"Tinoco, we can't fucking die like this, man. Not on Christmas, man! What the fuck is wrong with these people?"

"I know, Miles. We are not going to die, man. There is no fucking way we are going out on Christmas, fuck these motherfuckers!"

Those seconds and minutes felt like an eternity. We were both scared beyond belief. We had nothing to look at other than pitch-dark. The floodlights we had weren't much help at all, and the snow kept on falling as the red dots continued to move all over our heads, arms, our chests, and all around the inside of our tower.

The SOG kept talking to us all over the radio, trying to keep us calm. He sounded just as frantic as we were feeling.

After a few moments of us scanning out into darkness, our minds began to get the best of us. We seemed to be seeing movement out there; we just couldn't make out anything. Miles and I would shift abruptly every time we thought we caught movement. We were shitting bricks.

Five minutes passed, and nothing.

We kept mumbling crazy shit to each other. I think I began praying, and Miles followed suit shortly after. Snow kept on falling down on our faces as we quickly wiped it off our eyes, thinking it would impede our vision of the darkness in front of us. We still couldn't see anything.

Ten minutes passed; panic began to creep in. "What the hell is taking so long, man?"

"I don't know, Miles, but we're going to make it out of this, man. Just continue to talk to me."

"Tower Three, Tower Three!"

Someone was down below, calling for us.

Miles looked down and saw that it was one of the patrolling guards. "Yeah, we're still up here!"

"Hey, man, I'm coming up just didn't want you to shoot with everything that is going on."

"Okay, but you do so at your own risk. We are lit like fucking Christmas lights up here!"

The soldier made his way up to us and acknowledged our situation. "Holy shit, man."

"Help us scan for a possible target!"

He propped his rifle on the ledge of the tower and began to scan with us. "Shit, scan for what? I can't see a fucking thing out there."

The fact that this soldier walked up to us through the cover of darkness and the other structures around the camp gave me an idea.

"Miles, hand me the receiver and get a hold of the SOG."

"What? What the hell for?"

"Just do it, goddamit! Hand me the fucking receiver!"

I made contact with the SOG and asked if he could come over to

Tower Three.

"What the hell for, Tinoco?"

"Sarge, I have an idea that can help us deal with this shit a bit better."

He hesitated, and I'm sure he had a damn good reason for it. He really couldn't and wasn't supposed to leave his command post, especially in the situation we were in. The SOG's command post had direct communications with our brass and the scouts who were already out on patrol trying to figure out who the hell was targeting us.

Two minutes passed.

Three minutes.

Then I heard a voice from down below. "Hey, Tinoco. What the fuck do you want?"

It was the SOG. I quickly told Miles to man the .50 cal while I went down. He did so, but I could tell that he wasn't too pleased about doing so.

Once in the bottom, I expressed my idea to the SOG.

I told him how we could use two of the patrolling guards to go relieve one of the towers and then those two soldiers could maneuver toward the next tower and relieve those soldiers.

"This way, we all get a few minutes of relief from this madness of being targeted as we were making our way toward the next tower."

"I don't know, Tinoco."

"Sarge, look, I've been talking to you for at least three minutes and have actually been calm and not fearing for my life during these past three minutes! That is a lot of help and gives me hope that I am at least not being targeted right now!"

"I'll think about it!"

"Just go up to the tower, Sarge. You'll see how even one minute of relief will do a lot for us."

He finally agreed to join us on the tower for a minute. He did only stay for a minute before saying, "Okay, Tinoco; we are going to try this plan, but soldiers have to get to the next tower within five minutes!"

"Got it, Sarge!"

I'm sure that minute caused him to think of death and everything he was going to miss out on in life, his family back home; any future plans and goals were going to cease on that night if those laser dots were to be followed by bullets.

He quickly got off the tower and headed back to his post. A few minutes later, he was explaining "his idea" to us over the radio. He was going to send two patrolling guards to Tower One, and that would kick off the momentary relief for all of us.

It gave us hope to know that we were going to be relieved even if only for a few minutes.

Once the plan was set in motion, all of us were so relieved that we would actually make it to the next tower a lot faster than expected just so that we could keep it going as fast as possible and not torture ourselves waiting on the next relief.

This entire ordeal lasted for about forty-five minutes. In the end, the scouts were able to discover that Serbs had gone around to all the villages surrounding the camp and given little red laser toys to the kids in those villages.

The kids had been instructed by the Serbs to point those lasers at us during the night of Christmas Eve. They had done so, hoping to stir up an international incident led by American soldiers shooting down and killing a bunch of innocent kids.

I thank God every day that the Serbs were not successful in this endeavor. The possible headlines in the news are the least of my worries with regard to this matter.

The thought of mulling down a bunch of innocent kids with our .50-caliber machine guns would have been unbearable, and I am not certain I would be able to live with myself should that have taken place. I am forever grateful to the men I was with on that night and once again thank God for not letting any of us squeeze those triggers.

There was an incident that took place about two months later. This incident is clear and undeniable proof of the evil that exists in this world and lives among us. We all choose to do certain things for a reason. We are all believers of some greater being or greater cause that leads us to take certain actions or follow certain paths in our lives.

Unfortunately, in our world, the convictions of some can ultimately lead to the demise of others.

It was still fairly cold in Bosnia on this late February evening. Earlier that day, we had received news that the Serbs were once again preparing to plan an event that could lead to a serious international incident should our soldiers act outside the rules of engagement that were set for us.

I didn't think I had much to worry about since I hadn't been out on patrol again with any of our scouts or infantrymen and wasn't scheduled to join any patrol for some time. In my mind, I was safe within the confines of Camp Demi, doing my job as a logistician.

In the military, though, we are soldiers first and foremost.

I was sitting inside the camp cafeteria that evening, having dinner with other soldiers in my platoon, when our platoon sergeant approached us and informed us that a few of us might be going out of the wire later on.

All he knew at the moment was that it appeared to be a rescue mission of sorts. He said we would know more within the hour but asked for volunteers and suggested we all get our gear ready in case more of us were needed.

All of us at the table immediately said that we would volunteer. I don't think any of us even finished our meals. We all got up and went to our respective shacks to get the rest of our gear and await instructions from our platoon sergeant.

I got a few more items from my shack and went out toward the platoon sergeant's office; once I got there, the rest of the guys began trickling in as well. We were all part of the maintenance platoon, not combat-arms guys in any way, shape, or form. Yet we all wanted to make a difference in our own way somehow. We were all soldiers, and the guys that would be going out of the wire were our brethren as well.

A few minutes later, our platoon sergeant and the warrant officer showed up, along with the scouts' platoon sergeant. I was already somewhat close to the man since my actual job was to support his platoon and had already been out on patrol several times with them.

He said only four of us would be needed and then pointed directly at me. "You will be one of the four, Tinoco."

He told us all to link up with the rest of his men at the OPS shack in thirty minutes for a full brief and walked away. Our own platoon sergeant and chief looked at the four of us going and told us to be careful and follow all directions from the scouts. Twenty minutes later, all four of us were standing inside and in the back of the OPS shack.

The task seemed simple enough. Information had been collected indicating that Serbs were planning on burning down or blowing up the three remaining shelter homes for kids located about an hour away from our camp.

The three homes were known for sheltering Bosniak and Croatian kids whose families had been killed during their civil war. The Serbs were still trying to fulfill their own ethnic cleansing in the country.

There was no clear information on the timeline the Serbs had for implementing their devilish plans, but our instructions were clear. Reach the designated shelters, coordinate with the locals operating them and bring everyone back to camp. They would be evacuated to a safe location afterward. Two Humvees would be utilized for each of the three shelters along with a five-ton truck to be used for evacuating the kids and personnel.

Nothing to it.

The small unit I was placed in was in charge of going to the small town of Cerska, Bosnia. This town was known for having been brutally ravaged during the civil war by the Serbs. Several mass grave sites had already been located inside the town, and its people were doing what little they could just to recover from the atrocities that took place there. Now, because they had set up a shelter for kids, they were in danger of being targeted by Serbs again.

The staff sergeant with us kept repeating to us that our main goals were the clearing and evacuation of the shelter but to be prepared in case Serbs were in the area and decided to retaliate against us or the locals.

I don't think any of us wanted anything else to take place, nor did we want to get involved in anything else other than the rescue, but we were ready nonetheless.

The town of Cerska was only about an hour east of Camp Demi. The roads were rough and narrow for our Humvees, which always made for an interesting ride. One of our hummers had an M2 .50-caliber machine gun mounted on its turret, and the other one was mounted with an MK19 automatic grenade launcher. We were not taking any chances with such a small unit. Our five-ton cargo truck was positioned between both Hummers throughout the drive.

The staff sergeant leading our small unit kept calling out the time and distance to our location every ten minutes. Forty-five minutes into the drive, he called out something else.

"All right, men, time to get your game faces on; we are fifteen mikes out."

All of us had locked and loaded before we even left the safety perimeter of Camp Demi, but nothing ever truly gets a soldier's mind locked in to the possible dangers surrounding them like when the order to get your game face on comes through. When this happens, a new level of alertness and seriousness kicks in; everything and everyone is suspect.

"Entering the town of Cerska, men! We'll be at the shelter in less than five mikes! Be alert!"

Upon arriving at the shelter, one thought crossed my mind, *How the hell was this a shelter for kids?* It was a war-torn building with all its windows shattered, and from the outside, it didn't look like anyone could possibly live in it.

The place was surrounded by an old building that resembled a barn with part of its roof missing and a few battered houses. We positioned both Humvees on opposite corners in front of the shelter, and the five-ton was placed a few yards near the front door. Two other soldiers and I dismounted quickly from our Hummer while the driver and gunner remained on board. Security watch was primary and took place immediately as our SSG and interpreter made contact with the caretaker of the shelter. Five soldiers jumped off the back of the five-ton and began conducting security as well.

After about three minutes of discussion, our SSG centered himself from us and began calling out the two teams. Team One would provide security around the shelter and for the transport vehicle. Team Two would be making its way into the shelter and assist the caretaker with getting all the kids and his personnel on board the five-ton. The SSG would be leading all actions from outside and communicating back to base with progress reports as well.

I was part of Team Two.

"All right, men, let's get this done as quickly and safely as possible! Try not to scare the shit out of the kids!"

Four of us quickly ran into the shelter, along with our interpreter, and began ushering the older kids out first. The oldest couldn't have been more than thirteen years old. They were the easy ones; all we had to do was guide their movements toward the outside and onto the five-ton. We were all ushering six to seven kids out at a time.

We could see the fear in their eyes, the confusion, and worst—the sadness. This war-torn building had been home to them, and we were now forcing them out. I don't know if they had been told the reasons or if they even knew we were doing it for their own safety. The poor kids would quickly grab a few things from around their beds and rush toward us. Some grabbed filthy plush animals; some, torn, and other kids would grab a blanket and pillow that appeared to somehow be their safety nets and they couldn't leave without.

We had probably ushered two groups of kids out toward the five-ton when the gunfire began. All hell broke loose immediately. Glass shattered, and cement chips began to fly everywhere as bullets sprayed the outside and inside of the shelter. The noise inside was horrible as small items exploded around us because of the gunfire.

Then the most horrible sound I had ever heard erupted all around us. The simultaneous crying and yelling of little kids, boys and girls alike yelling at the top of their lungs. The noise was deafening. I couldn't hear the gunfire anymore; all I kept hearing were their ear-piercing cries. I tried to push through their cries to listen to my fellow soldiers as they kept moving around me in an attempt to protect as many kids as possible.

Our movements inside the shelter were swift and, in a way, numb—numb to the chaos surrounding us at the moment. It was as if all of us inside didn't care for our own lives and well-being; we had all somehow made the simultaneous decision that the lives of those kids mattered more. They were the mission, and we had to trust in our own buddies outside to take care of the hostile element that had just decided to alter our plans.

To our shocking surprise, there were a handful of toddlers and infants in the building as well. We quickly began to pick up two at a time and crawl along the various walls, beds, tables, and anything else that could provide some form of cover from the gunfire as we made our way toward the exit.

I had two toddlers with me (they must have been about three or four years old) , when I arrived at the exit. Two other soldiers were already there, waiting for the right time to rush out toward the five-ton. The screaming and crying wouldn't stop cutting through all the other racket surrounding us. The soldier nearest to the door took a look outside and yelled, "Running out with kids!"

He was holding a toddler and a baby! A baby! Did the fucking Serbs not know what they were shooting at? Did they not care? Someone outside, I believe the SSG, yelled out for our buddies to cover fire. As soon as the order was given, a thunderous sound erupted from our soldiers' weapons. This gave the two soldiers in front of me the opportunity to run out with the kids. They must have run at the speed of light because they were back inside the shelter a moment later and crouching near me now.

Specialist Miller had made his way toward me with two other toddlers as well. As the first two soldiers crawled their way back toward the middle of the shelter to look for more kids, I yelled out that we were running out with kids as well. Thunder erupted again, and we ran like hell toward the five-ton, quickly handing the kids over to the personnel already on the truck, and dashed back into the shelter. When Miller and I made it back inside, the caretaker and our interpreter were near the doorway.

Specialist Miller crouched next to the interpreter and began to yell, "We need him to show us where the rest of the kids are!" Both the interpreter and the caretaker were shaking frantically; the fear was eating away at them.

The caretaker was pretty much done. The shock of the whole ordeal was paralyzing him in a moment when we needed him the most. Specialist Miller crawled toward him and slapped the shit out of him. The caretaker just stared. Miller slapped him again, harder. This time, the caretaker woke up.

"Are there any more kids inside, and how do we get to them?"

The caretaker started to stand up, and I immediately shoved his ass back toward the floor. We were still taking fire from what seemed like every direction. I began signaling and yelling at the caretaker to move crouched down toward the floor. He seemed to have gotten the idea because he nodded his head, indicating that he understood, and began crawling toward other rooms inside the shelter. We must have checked four rooms that had already been emptied. As we were making our way into the fifth and last room, we came across the other two soldiers in the hallway. Miller informed them that there was one more room that needed to be checked, so they followed closely behind us.

At the entrance of that last room was an old lady lying on the floor, dead. Inside the room were two other adult females, also dead. One of them was leaning over a crib that had been turned over, probably from her own weight as she collapsed after being hit. About five feet away from her was the other lady. All three ladies had died trying to save the kids inside that room. I saw a total of about seven dead kids lying near and around these last two ladies. All were dead.

We all just stopped there, momentarily taking it all in and trying to convince ourselves that what we were seeing was just not possible. Kids, innocent kids whose only crime was being born to a part of the world that did not want them to live. The entire scene was surreal.

It was the caretaker who broke our paralyzed state of being this time around. He began tugging at my shoulder and signaling to the outside as I snapped out of it and acknowledged what he was telling me.

I began to shout at Miller and the other guys, "Miller! Miller! We have to get the hell out of here, man! There is nothing more we can do here! They're dead, they're all dead!"

But Miller wasn't snapping out of it.

I kept on repeating myself and had to maneuver toward all the bodies, one at a time, and check to see if any had survived that horrific scene to make sure the guys could acknowledge and accept that we couldn't do anything else for the ladies and the kids inside that room.

Even now, I don't know how I was able to numb myself in order to check those kids without breaking down. All I can think is that my survival instinct had taken over, and all that mattered to me at that moment was to get everybody out of the building and get to a position where we could actually fight back.

Finally, one of the other guys snapped back to reality and assisted me with the rest. We began pushing everybody out toward the hallway again so that we could make our way to the exit. The place kept on exploding around us. As we were nearing the exit, we all heard a loud scream and immediately turned toward it.

The caretaker had been shot and was now lying in a fetal position, holding on to his shoulder. Miller and I quickly got to him and asked where else he was shot. Thankfully, it was just his shoulder. We grabbed him and got him near the door. Miller instructed the other two scouts to cover fire for us as we took the caretaker to the five-ton. One of the scouts, the one closest to the exit, peeked out to gage where our guys were and where the gunfire was coming from.

His reaction was unexpected in the midst of all the chaos. He snapped back up against the wall and just looked at us all. He started mouthing something, but we couldn't make out his words. I don't think any sound was coming out of his mouth, to be honest.

I let go of the caretaker momentarily and pulled on the scout's frag vest. "What is it? What the fuck did you see?"

Nothing was coming out; he just looked at me. His eyes looked confused, scared, shocked, yet he also had a look of extreme concern about him that I could not understand.

"Man, shake it the fuck off; we have to move out of here and link up with the rest of our guys!"

I shook him a few more times and finally got through to him. "They're kids, man, they're fucking kids!"

I heard him but didn't fully understand what was being said. I figured he was still having a tough time accepting the fact that these assholes were outside trying to kill all those kids and had been successful with a few of them.

I grabbed his weapon and shoved it onto his chest. "Get ready, we are heading out together!"

I looked at Miller and the rest of the guys, and somehow they understood that we were about to run out of there. Miller immediately chimed in, "Be careful what you shoot at as we run out, we don't want to hit our own guys!"

He got close to me and yelled out toward the outside, "We're running out, cover fire!"

It sounded as though the entire world were collapsing around us with all the gunfire sounding off everywhere. Miller and I grabbed hold of the caretaker, and we all ran out toward the five-ton together, firing away as we did so. We quickly tossed the interpreter and the caretaker onto the truck, closed the tailgate, and began taking positions with the rest of our guys.

I saw Miller make his way toward the staff sergeant, and a moment later, he was checking around to ensure he could account for all of us. Once he was satisfied with his count, he began to signal and yell out for all to mount up and move on out; he would be the lead.

The MK19 unloaded a barrage of grenades all around our area to cover for us as we all mounted back onto our vehicles. The smoke, debris, and dust that was being blasted sky-high became our immediate concealment as we mounted up and began doing our own headcount inside the vehicles.

The staff sergeant asked over the radio, "Is everyone up!"

Miller responded from my Humvee, and then the passenger of the five-ton responded as well. We were all up. "Okay, let's go, let's go, let's go!"

Gunfire continued as we hauled ass out of there; the sounds of bullets hitting our armored vehicles became our measure in estimating that we had cleared the area a few moments later. The farther we got, the fewer pings we heard slam against our vehicles. We could hear the staff sergeant calling out to base and letting them know we were en route but had taken heavy fire on-site. Some moron at base actually advised us to be cautious the rest of the way since it was unknown if we would encounter any other resistance on the road.

Our gunner immediately yelled out, "No fucking shit, asshole!" Luckily, he wasn't the one holding the radio mic.

I don't think any of us said a single word all the way back to Camp Demi. I don't think any of us even felt relaxed or safe until we were inside the wire again. I know that, as soon as we drove into the camp, I let out a huge sigh of relief and got off the Humvee as soon as we stopped.

Everyone followed suit, and we all checked one another out for signs of blood and asked one another if we were okay. The adrenaline was just now beginning to subside, and the exhaustion would follow shortly after. The other units had already been inside the wire for quite some time. Apparently, the unit I was with had been the only one that encountered any resistance.

The following days and nights were troublesome. Throughout the day, I would keep my mind occupied with work and would look for anything extra to do that would help keep me busy. I couldn't sleep well at night because I kept thinking of the poor dead kids and the grotesquely stupid reason they had been killed for. Religion. How could anyone end an innocent kid's life simply because of a difference in religious beliefs?

What made matters worse was the fact that several of the soldiers from my team that were involved in the rescue would come up to me and let me know about their thoughts, nightmares, and difficulties they were having. I would remain quiet and listen to them as they began rehashing everything they saw that evening. I was allowing them to voice their fears while, at the same time, I was suppressing my own sorrows.

I felt that I had to remain strong for them. They had somehow found it easy to confide in me and to believe that I would somehow guide them through their own torment. I felt obligated to do just that, and I couldn't let them see that I was having the same problems. I had to demonstrate that I was stronger, that I could listen to their issues, and that I could pass on a few words that could, hopefully, help them throughout the days and nights that followed.

I used to think that the need or desire to be there for the other soldiers was stronger than my own concerns, thoughts, and bad dreams. I used to think that, by being strong and being there for them, my own problems would somehow vanish and allow me to be the same "normal-functioning" soldier I had always been.

Man, was I ever so wrong.

I was once again going out on patrol with a few grunts when I wasn't supposed to. I mean, I had gotten approval through my chain of command, but I really never had any business going on all these patrols. I had even been given a direct order from our local medical staff to not be doing anything crazy anymore.

This was due to the fact that a landmine had blown up a British soldier about ten yards from me and the force of the blast had slammed me against an M113A3 medic track . The hit was pretty rough, I had hurt my neck, back, knees, and nose.

We had just arrived on location to relieve the British soldiers in clearing a minefield that was discovered earlier that day. I remember us cracking jokes about the task on our way to the site because, back then, we would actually probe for mines by sticking a metal rod into the ground. As crazy as this sounds, what was even crazier was having to still go out and assist on clearing that minefield after the explosion. Talk about being forced to literally "shake it off" and go looking for mines after seeing another soldier get blown up to pieces on that same field.

This last patrol with the grunts of our unit led us toward a mass gravesite that had been discovered in the outskirts of Cerska, the same little town where we had rescued the kids. We had been told by upper management that our role on-site would be to provide security for the NATO soldiers, their medical personnel, and the local populace that would be there. I had never been a part of such tasking and truly did not know what I was getting myself into.

It turned out that none of us did.

Upon making our way to the site, I remember walking over with the sergeant in charge of us and linking up with a NATO officer. The smell of the place was horrible. Wrapping cloths around our noses and mouths did not help at all. The smell of decaying death was so pungent that there was no getting around it. It only took me about three minutes before I began throwing-up what food I had in me. Once I began, other soldiers followed suit and blew chunks around our vehicles.

The mass gravesite was a huge crater in the ground. Looking into it and around it, I was shocked not only by the smell of it, but also by the way all the bodies were just piled up. The NATO officer and our sergeant had taken a few steps away from me, but I could still hear what was being said. Our initial role was to provide security while the NATO soldiers and medical staff were supposed to be getting the bodies out of the crater and lining them up for the local populace to come over to try to identify them. I could see that a whole lot of bodies had already been lined up away from the crater, and the locals were eerily walking over them in search of their loved ones.

I say *eerily* because it appeared as though they were already used to this sort of thing. It was as if they were just fulfilling another daily task that had to be done throughout the day. There were some folks grieving out loud as they found their family members, but for the most part, everyone was just walking around, looking at the bodies in a numbed state of being. I couldn't understand how all this was somehow "normal" to them.

Well, it turned out that our roles had changed. The NATO soldiers were pulling out of the area, and it was up to us now to get the bodies out of the crater and line them up for the locals to identify.

"Who is going to pull security for us, Sarge?"

"Nobody! We are!"

"We are?"

"Yes, half of us will pull bodies out while the other half conducts security operations."

None of us could believe what we were hearing, yet we had to do as we were told. Griping and bitching, we all gathered as the sergeant appointed half of us for getting the bodies out and the other half to pull security.

I wasn't an infantryman or a member of their platoon, so of course, I was stuck getting bodies. I remember the sergeant telling me that I would be in charge of my group. I think he was trying to make up for the fact that I was given that shit duty. In any case, being placed in charge only made matters worse for me.

For this particular assignment, I was given seven soldiers, making us a team of eight. The even number of soldiers was necessary for the collecting of bodies. Most of us gagged and blew chunks again prior to making our way down into the crater. We even tried to look for smelly leaves or grass to place near our nostrils to cover the stench, but it seemed as though the smell of death had gotten into everything that was nearby. All we could do was wait for the moment when we would get used to the putrid smell. I don't think that moment ever came, but the task of getting bodies out of the hole in the ground sure made us forget all about the smell.

Having been placed in charge, I felt it necessary to be one of the first guys to grab a body and pull it out. I signaled one of the other soldiers and asked him to join me. I remember offering him the choice of whether to grab legs or torso; the guy chose legs, of course. The ground was wet and muddy, which only made things that much more difficult for us. We approached the body nearest to us and assumed our positions on opposite ends. I crouched and tried to somehow hook my hands underneath the body's arms while my partner grabbed hold of its legs. I looked at my partner and said, "On three."

"One, two, three!" and we both heaved the body upward toward our waists. What happened next was unbearable and unforgettable.

On my end, the head of the body broke off or was already off; in any case, it remained on the ground as I lifted. On my partner's end, he lifted the legs, and they came undone from the rest of the body. We simultaneously looked down at the remains and then looked at each other in disbelief. A second later, we were both throwing up again next to the body.

After a few moments of throwing up whatever we had left inside us, I looked over at my partner again and told him we would have to take out the body in pieces.

"Are you fucking serious?"

"Dude, how else are we going to get this done? If all the bodies come apart like this one, we will have to get them out of here in pieces. It sucks ass, I know, but we have to."

"Well, that's just fucking great!"

I waited for him to compose himself before moving toward the body again. I remember looking at my partner and then just willed myself to grab what I could of the torso and carry it out of the crater. After placing the torso on the ground in line with the rest, I made my way back to the crater and saw that my partner was already making his way out with the legs and the head. I had to help him though with all the mud on the ground, there was no way we would be making any quick progress on this. I looked around the crater and searched for an easier path up, but it was all the same.

"Okay, guys, it looks like we may have to play the chain game on this. Let's line up, and we'll pass the bodies to each other, upward and out of this crater."

After seeing what my partner and I had gone through, everyone quickly agreed that it would be the best course of action. We all lined up in pairs just in case some of the bodies did remain intact, and began the dreadful process of removing as many bodies as possible from the crater. We only managed a few bodies before two of the soldiers began freaking out. All the bodies we had grabbed so far had broken apart on our hands; this was making the entire ordeal that much more unbearable.

Seeing what it was doing to us mentally, I decided to tell the guys to take a break, get out, and look away from the crater. Unfortunately for all of us, the sobbing and crying of some of the families that had already identified the bodies that were lined up were adding to our own anguish. We had been out of the crater for about three minutes when the sergeant came over to us and asked what the hell was going on. Why had we stopped? I did explain to him how the bodies were in bad shape and were falling apart as we tried to carry them out of the mass grave. I told him that we all just needed a few minutes away from it all to regain our own composure and that we would get back to it. It was clear that the sergeant didn't care, nor did he want to listen to our "excuses" for taking a break from it all.

"I don't give a shit what you have to do or what you all have to tell each other, but these bodies will be taken out of this hole today. The quicker you quit being little bitches about this matter, the quicker you can get it done so that we can all get out of here!"

I could not believe what this man was telling me. We did not even have a medical staff to help with the bodies in any way. We were all struggling with the limbs and torsos to get them out of the hole they were in, and the rest of the guys were having an even-tougher time ensuring the bodies were put together accordingly. We couldn't rush the process for fear of mismatching limbs, torsos, and heads. The entire process was sickening, frustrating, infuriating, and mentally exhausting.

As the hours passed, some of the guys continued to complain about the entire process, and the act of talking one another past the unpleasantness of it all only led to arguing among us. The bickering among the guys was getting worse by the minute. The fact that we kept on stopping from time to time in order to maintain our own sanity was not helping us much. On our last break, half of the guys said they couldn't continue. I had to go over to the sergeant and ask him if he could replace us with the guys who were pulling security.

"I'm not exposing any more of my soldiers to this shit! This task is yours and yours alone! Just fucking make it happen, Tinoco!"

I wanted to beat the crap out of him; how could he not see how this was affecting us all? We needed relief, and we were not about to get any from anyone. As I walked back toward my guys, having worked together on that one hellish task—hell yes, they were my guys—I guess they saw the disappointment on my face, because they were more upset when I finally reached them.

"The sarge isn't going to switch us out, is he?"

"No, he's not. Says this is all ours and doesn't want any other soldier exposed to this bullshit."

"So it's okay for all of us to get mind-fucked like this but not for others?"

"Look, man, it's understandable. Just think about it. We have already been doing this crap all day. Do you really wish this shit on anyone else?"

Silence.

"We have to finish this. Fucking NATO soldiers left us with their job and didn't even have the decency to help us out with some medical personnel to piece the bodies back together again."

"That shit isn't right, Tinoco!"

"No. It isn't right, but the only option we have is to finish this job and get the hell out of here. So let's get to it."

I guess the local folks around us had noticed that we were arguing, and some old man came over to us, holding a large black bag. The bag was made out of some thick plastic. I was a bit puzzled at first but quickly figured out what it was once the old man started pointing at the bodies inside the crater and then at the bodies already lined up outside.

They were actual body bags. I took the bag from him and began gesturing for more by pointing at the bag and then visually counting with my fingers, hoping that he would get the idea that I needed more bags. The old man smiled right away and walked off toward a huge sack lying on the ground at the head of the lined-up bodies. With all the dead bodies surrounding us and the dreadful task of pulling them out of the crater, I had never noticed that sack before. The old man pulled out several bags from it and raised them to show me that we did have a bunch of bags.

I went over to the old man, thanked him by patting his back and shaking his hand, grabbed the entire sack of bags, and took it back toward the crater. I took some out and began instructing the guys that we would place the bodies inside the bags so that it would be easier to pull them out of the crater. Half of the guys were ready to begin working again, while the other half was still hesitating and griping about our task.

I repeated myself and saw that I was getting nowhere with the guys complaining.

I lost it.

"Look! I don't want to hear your bitching. We are all in this shit together, and we have no choice but to get it done. So get your asses back into the crater and start putting the bodies in the bags. Your griping is not making this any easier, and you're only making this ordeal longer than it has to be!"

I don't think the guys were expecting me to lash out at them. They stood there momentarily, possibly trying to figure out if I was serious enough to actually make them do what needed to be done or not. I walked up directly in front of two of them and made sure they realized I meant business.

"You can do this on your own, or I can throw your asses into the hole! It's your fucking choice. Either way, your asses will be inside this crater, pulling bodies out with the rest of us!"

The guys gave one last sigh of frustration before taking the bags from me and moving back into the crater. None of us said a thing for the next two hours or so. We just kept grabbing body after body, placing them in bags and then hauling them out of the crater. We were all raging inside, and you could sense it among us. We just kept on pushing through the madness of it all until every last body was out of the mass gravesite.

The closer we got to the bottom of the crater, the worse the decayed bodies were. Yet none of us threw up anymore. I think we all somehow figured out a way to numb our own thoughts and emotions about the whole ordeal and finally got to the point where the deadly stench wasn't affecting us anymore. To be honest, I don't think I even heard the locals crying either; I had somehow tuned them out as well.

Upon hauling the last bag full of limbs and bones out, we all made our way out of the crater and just walked away. We didn't look at one another, didn't say a word to one another; we simply walked away toward our vehicles, and I don't think any of us bothered to look back toward the lined-up body bags or the crater.

It took me a few moments to regain my thoughts and finally walk over toward the sergeant in charge of us. When I got to him, I don't remember saying anything. I just stood there looking at him, and for the life of me, I can't remember if he said anything to me. The next thing I knew, he was on the radio, letting our headquarters know that the task was complete and asking if we could head back to base.

None of the guys I was riding with talked at all. It was probably the most silent ride I had ever been on. I think I lost myself on that ride back to base because I don't recall thinking anything or looking at anything the entire way back. It was as if I were not even inside that Humvee, and I can't exactly say where I was mentally; that ride back has been lost to me ever since.

The aftermath of this tasking was just like that of the rescue mission. The guys that I had worked with on that dreadful day kept on coming over to me for guidance or to simply get their thoughts out and have someone listen to them. I don't know why I did, but I kept on trying to be the strong one for them. I never shared my own thoughts, feelings, or troubles with them. In my mind, they were already struggling with their own thoughts and feelings, so why burden them with mine? Not only that, I knew that I would need those guys again in some other patrol or mission, and I needed them to believe I would be there for them should the need arise.

They needed to know that they could depend on me, and I needed to know that they would follow me.

To make matters worse, I didn't feel that I could go talk to my own platoon sergeant or my own chief about what I was going through or experiencing. So I did what I knew best and overwhelmed myself with work and with exercising. The gym on base was open 24-7, and I was there whenever I wasn't working or listening to the other soldiers' problems.

I was having problems with my own emotions and didn't know how to contain them or deal with them, so I would just work and exercise until I collapsed with exhaustion. I felt I needed it in order to get some sleep because that too had become an issue for me. I would just lie awake all night, lost in my own thoughts and fears.

Our deployment was finally coming to an end, and I was afraid of facing my son for the first time. I had been absent for most of his first year of life, and I was afraid that I was no longer the same person. I was afraid of not being able to feel anything after struggling those last few months with suppressing whatever emotions I felt.

I should have seen back then how my listening to the other soldiers had helped them somewhat. I should have seen and recognized how allowing the soldiers to voice their own issues to me had somehow made things easier for them to cope with. I didn't, though; I couldn't. I was so consumed by my own thoughts and fears that I couldn't see things as clearly as I should have.

Leaving Bosnia and Herzegovina was confusing to me. I wanted to leave the place and get as far away from anything that reminded me of the things I had done and seen there. I wanted to get back to some form of normalcy, yet I didn't think I was ready to go home. I wanted to get home, but I was also afraid of doing so. The confusion was overwhelming.

During any deployment, soldiers get to see other soldiers struggle with events that are taking place back home. Some soldiers lose loved ones by way of separation or divorce. Others experience the death of a family member or a dear friend. Seeing one another go through such trials and tribulations during a deployment only adds to your own grief. You do what you can to be there for your brethren, and they, in turn, do the same for you. What makes these events a living hell is that we are on the other side of the world, with no power to do anything about it. The struggle to cope or accept matters only worsens because we have to set those thoughts and feelings aside to continue doing our jobs. We can't allow family or relationship issues hinder our performance. Otherwise, we would be placing our brethren's lives at risk.

So yes, getting on that plane to return home does bring all those personal issues to the forefront. Thinking you're flying back to a shattered home can be a debilitating experience. Mostly everyone around you is excited and happy to be returning home while you may not even know what you're returning to. Unfortunately, this was exactly what I was experiencing. I knew I was returning to an estranged wife and a son I hadn't met yet. I knew I was going back home to face another challenge. I wasn't going home to relax and enjoy all the things I had missed so much.

I was on the last flight back to the United States. All the other soldiers from my shop had already arrived. I remember the nervousness of the entire flight. We didn't want any accidents to take place, any malfunctions. It sure was something to hear the thunder that erupted within the plane when our pilot notified us all that he was about to begin his descend toward the West Fort Hood Airport.

The entire plane immediately filled up with whistling, yelling, hollering, and soldiers cheering for having made it back safely. It was an amazing moment. About twenty minutes later, another thundering roar took place as we all felt the tires of the plane touch down on the airstrip. I felt my skin fill up with goose bumps from the nervous excitement and my entire being swell up with the overwhelming emotions that rushed through me at that moment. We were home!

Our emotions continued to intensify as the pilot once again got on the intercom to thank us all for our service and to be the first in saying "Welcome home!"

Getting off the plane was pretty surreal. The First Cavalry Regiment Band was outside, playing, as we made our way onto the buses that would take us to our respective units. We were headed to the Iron Horse Gym, which was located across the street from our battalion headquarters and barracks. We sang cadence all the way to the gym. Our buses must have woken up all of Fort Hood with all the noise we were making. Seeing all the familiar buildings and landmarks of the base sure was a sight for sore eyes. I don't think there was a dry eye on my bus, and the same was probably true for all the other buses that night.

Outside the gym parking lot were a few sergeants waiting for our buses to stop and instruct us to form up so that we could be marched into the gym. This was a bit strange because, aside from the instructions being barked out at us, we couldn't hear anything else. It was quiet, too quiet. After we were all formed up, the NCOs began marching us toward the double doors of the gym, where several soldiers were standing by.

As soon as the doors were opened and the first soldiers of our formation stepped into the gym, the song "Proud to Be an American" by Lee Greenwood exploded through speakers that had been set up inside the gym. People inside the gym began clapping and hollering at our formation as we marched inside. I don't know about the other soldiers, but my emotions were so overwhelming I was actually choking up trying to contain them. I saw many of the people inside were also singing the song as it played on, and they too were all teary-eyed as they were overcome by their own feelings.

When the song ended, our national anthem began to play. The gym silenced as we all listened to the music and words of our anthem while the people standing on the bleachers in front of us all placed their hands across their chests and on their hearts.

I was sobbing, drowning in my thoughts and feelings as I listened and remembered that cold Christmas Eve. I remembered how the other soldiers and I had actually believed we were not going to make it home.

I thought of the landmine that had blown up near me and taken the life of a NATO soldier. I couldn't contain my tears at all as thoughts of the kids we had saved took over me and shook me to the core.

I remember struggling to contain myself, but the national anthem had taken over me; it had overpowered my entire being, and I could do nothing about it. I thanked *God*, yet I also asked for forgiveness. Forgiveness for not being able to save all the kids that night. Forgiveness for having to shoot back and taking the lives of others who had been conditioned to hate us for no reason other than not sharing the same faith. I begged *God* for forgiveness because I had cursed him so many times in my sleepless nights as I asked and asked for answers while I felt that I had not received any. Lastly, I cried more as I thanked Him for allowing me to come back home and be able to see my son.

All these thoughts and feelings of despair, grief, anger, joy, and relief ran through me at once, crippling me as I stood there in the position of attention.

When the national anthem ended, our battalion commander began to speak. I began scanning through all the people in the gym, trying to locate my own family. I don't remember a word that was said. I was too busy looking for my family and becoming disheartened with every passing second that I couldn't locate them. Had my fears of coming back home to an estranged family been correct?

The commander continued his speech, and I continued my search as discouragement began to sink in. I do remember seeing the commander turn around toward the families and letting them know it was okay for them to step down and welcome their soldiers. In that moment, he released us all and only asked that we turn in our weapons after seeing our families. Apparently, somewhere in his speech, he had given us a four-day weekend, and I hadn't even heard it.

Our formation broke, and everyone dispersed in search of their family members. I stood there still and continued to scan. I must have scanned for about ten more minutes and then finally gave up searching. I hadn't seen my family and began to make my way toward the exit. My gloom only grew as I heard all the cheerful sobbing among the other soldiers and their families. Witnessing all the hugs and kisses among them all was beginning to be too much for me as I kept on walking toward the exit. As I reached for the door, I stopped and forced myself to turn and look through the crowd one last time.

My son! I rushed over to my family, and my son Mark somehow just knew me. I was still a few steps away from them, and he was already reaching out for me. I paused as I reached them for some reason. I could feel something there; a barrier of sorts was definitely standing between my wife and me, but my son just smiled and reached out for me as though we had been together all this time. I took him and hugged him as he giggled and smiled at me. Oh, what a moment that was. In that moment, I forgot the entire world. I was holding my son for the first time ever. We just kept on looking at each other as I held him and smiled with him. Somehow, someway, I was not a stranger to him. That night, after turning-in my weapon and going to a local hotel, I just played with him but mostly just admired him. I had longed to have him with me for so long and on a few occasions even questioned if that day would actually come. It's strange to say, but playing with Mark and looking at him sort of placed me in a peaceful trance. Nothing around me seemed to even exist during that first night. Even after my son was sound asleep, all I did was look at him; I was lost somehow.

My wife had already told me, before my flight back, that she and the baby were going to continue living with her parents. No matter what points I had made while deployed in all our conversations, I could not change her mind. I think that seeing her for the first time again and truly sensing that barrier that had been built between us made me realize the cold fact that I had lost my family. Accepting that reality was tough, but it allowed me to just focus on my son. I wanted to enjoy every moment with him. I wanted to ensure he knew I was his father. I didn't want him to grow up looking for role models in other men. I wanted to be his first and best role model. I was scared, but something about the peace he made me feel gave me hope that I could push through it all.

I was wrong.

On my way to work in Camp Demi, Bosnia

PR work with some of the locals in the villages
surrounding Camp Demi, Bosnia

Driving through the city of Sarajevo, Bosnia

A landmine exploded near me about five
minutes after this picture was taken.

What remained of an old observatory in Sarajevo, Bosnia

Driving through the war torn city of Sarajevo, Bosnia, near the airport

Chevrons

· · · · · · · · · · · · · · · · · · · ·

The first few months of being back from Bosnia were rough. I had to beg to see my son. Nothing seemed to be going well at all with my personal life. Divorce was becoming the inevitable option with every passing day.

I have to say that the one thing that kept me grounded and focused was my job. Our shop had gained new leadership, and I was being looked at for a promotion as well. Prior to our deployment, I had been able to attend the army Primary Leadership Development Course. The training took place at Fort Hood. It is a monthlong course that places army specialists and corporals in situations that demand a take-charge attitude of them. Soldiers are trained and mentored on how to effectively lead small groups of soldiers. The training is broken down to focus on several leadership skills, such as map reading, land navigation, war fighting, drill and ceremony, and of course, leadership.

My buddy Jack had encouraged me to attend and helped me prepare for the training. He knew I was being looked at for promotion, and although he had more time in service than I did, he somehow believed that I would do well as a sergeant. I still remember how nervous I had been on the day of my promotion board. Both Jack and Sergeant Bess were doing their best to hype me up and get me in the right mind-set prior to sitting down in front of the board members. The board was comprised of all the company first sergeants and the command sergeant major of the battalion. The reason for my being nervous was the fact that it was commonly known the board members were not too keen on promoting individuals who were not "combat arms." The CSM was the individual leading that mind-set and could not understand why a logistics soldier was even being considered for promotion. This is one of the drawbacks of being a support element; sometimes, the leadership does not see you as one of their own.

Jack, Sergeant Bess, and I were all standing outside the CSM's office, waiting to be called in. Sergeant Bess had already informed me that he would be called in first so that he could let the board know a bit about me and why he felt I was ready to wear chevrons and lead soldiers.

"You have to go in that room pissed off at all the board members, Tinoco. Some of those assholes don't think you're ready. Prove them wrong! Show them what you are made of, and make them all go fuck themselves!"

This was Jack doing his best in motivating me. Jack was always a very vocal person, and he had already seen some of the struggles I had gone through with regard to management not caring for a support element soldier or not understanding why someone like me could be held in such high regard by the combat arms soldiers.

Then Sergeant Bess chimed in, "That's right, Tinoco. You have to walk in there knowing that the chevrons are already yours and those assholes are trying to take them from you. Do not let them do that! You can't let them do that!"

By the time they were done hyping me up, I was ticked off. All the nervousness I had been feeling somehow washed away, and I couldn't wait to go into that promotion board and give them a piece of my mind. Funny thing is that I believe Jack felt I was too hyped up and now needed to be calmed down. It is a strange feeling for someone to get you all roused up and ready to kick some ass only to have that same person try to calm you down a minute afterward. I can still remember Jack's "holy shit" expression when he realized I might actually walk into the board and tell everyone to fuck off.

Sergeant Bess had already been called in, and for the next five minutes, Jack did his best to calm me down again. The thing is, he couldn't or didn't want me to be completely relaxed; he still wanted me to be somewhat aggressive, so his coaching had to have a very delicate balance. How he figured that shit out, I don't know.

A few minutes later, Sergeant Bess opened the door and instructed me on what to do next. I had to knock on the door hard and wait for someone to say "Come in." Once inside, I had to make my way to the front of the board members, center myself, salute, and announce myself to the board members. I had to wait for the CSM to return my salute and then continue standing at the position of attention until told to sit down by the CSM. This was done so that all the board members could take a close look at my dress uniform and ensure that I had every medal and accessory in its correct place. The CSM gave me a few facing movements to get a glimpse at my entire uniform and once everyone was pleased, I was instructed to take a seat.

I remember introducing myself to all the board members, ensuring I made eye contact with everyone throughout my introduction. The final statement of my introduction needed to be my reasoning for wanting to become a leader in the United States Army and what my long-term goal was. For this, I looked directly at the CSM and told him that I felt I could do great things for the army as a leader and felt that I could get soldiers to follow me through any situation. For my long-term goal, I paused and told him, "I want your job, Command Sergeant Major!"

By the look on his face, I don't think he was expecting me to say that I wanted to have his job. He was probably expecting some vague answer that only addressed leadership in general terms. With that done, he went down the line asking the other board members if they had any questions for me.

All of them said they had no questions to ask of me and that they were pleased to see how I always carried myself at work. The CSM was not pleased at all.

"Well, I guess your work ethic and reputation precedes you, Specialist

Tinoco. I am actually surprised to see that none of my first sergeants have anything to ask you."

He took another look at all the board members, as if asking, "Are you all serious?"

"Okay, Specialist Tinoco, your promotion board hearing has ended. We will let your squad leader, Sergeant Bess, know how you did. You may excuse yourself."

With that said, I stood up at the position of attention once more, saluted, thanked the CSM and all the first sergeants for the opportunity, and waited for the CSM to return my salute. Once done, I did a facing movement and marched out of the office. Jack was still outside waiting, and he was in shock to see I had finished so quickly.

"What the hell happened, Tinoco? How did it go?"

"Bro, I think it went great because none of the first sergeants asked me anything!"

"What?"

"Yeah, bro. Not a single question was asked. And I don't think the command sergeant major liked it all, but there was nothing he could do! I think it pissed him off, and I told his ass that I wanted his job!"

"What? You are fucking crazy, man!"

Then Sergeant Bess walked out of the office with a big, old grin on his face. He signaled us to walk away from the office. He didn't want us making a lot of noise. He stopped us and looked directly at me. "Hey, Jackson, would you believe that we are now looking at the future Sergeant Tinoco?"

Man, I jumped for joy at the statement. I high-fived and hugged both of them. I was elated. I was going to get chevrons. I was going to lead soldiers. Me! The poor migrant worker from Weslaco, Texas, had just been told that the United States Army wanted him to be a leader of soldiers! Never in my wildest dreams during all those years of picking crops had I seen this coming. Never had I expected that one day, people who I saw as my leaders and mentors would ask me to join their ranks and help them lead soldiers through whatever obstacles the military threw at us.

In that moment, hearing that news and sharing it with Jack was one of the greatest feelings in the world for me. Little did I know that becoming the sergeant and leader of soldiers was going to be so rewarding yet so debilitating. The pride that came with that promotion did not come close to the responsibility it entailed.

I wasn't promoted until after my deployment to Bosnia, and by then, Jack had left the 2/5 Cavalry Regiment and was now working with another support battalion. In any case, I don't think I could have ever earned my chevrons without his guidance and words of encouragement. No matter what I was going through, I always knew I could count on Jack, my black red-headed brother.

So why do I say that becoming a leader in the military can be debilitating? Some of it has to do with all the things I went through in Bosnia. Even though I was not wearing chevrons yet, I was being there for the soldiers who would come up to me and express their fears, nightmares, and at times, even thoughts of hopelessness. Somehow, my words of encouragement allowed them all to carry on with their duties and gave them the courage or heart to continue moving forward. I didn't know that my actions were those of what other soldiers saw as leadership. That reality didn't sink in until way after I had been pinned with my chevrons and was officially leading soldiers. And even then, it took for me to listen to soldiers tell their parents and wives that they would follow me through hell for me to actually realize what I was doing.

That statement carries a lot of weight and responsibility. Not only does one have to worry about the soldiers and the mission, but now one also has to worry about not letting the soldiers' family members down since they are being told that you will get their loved ones back from any mission they ever get sent to. Granted, the few times I was in tough situations, like all other soldiers, I just reacted to those particular events. One doesn't sit back and think of these matters until after everything has transpired. In my particular case, it has taken me years to see and somewhat understand things for what they were.

My promotion to sergeant and my window for reenlistment opening up after the deployment were exactly what I needed to keep my mind occupied on something else other than the hard time I was having with my wife. I believe these things kept me sane to a certain extent and prevented me from falling into a dark state of hopelessness and depression. Unfortunately, I was also starting to drink heavily.

Having a few good laughs at a military ball

Germany

• • • • • • • • • • • • • • • • • • • •

For my final reenlistment in the army, I had actually requested to be sent back to Kosovo. Our military had begun bombing the place while I was still in Bosnia and the search for the Yugoslavian president Slobodan Milošević had been initiated. This man was also known as the president of the Serbian Republic and had long initiated his own ethnic-cleansing program in Kosovo.

Many may wonder why a soldier would want to go back into the same chaotic state of being that has caused so many nightmares. I truly don't know the answer to that. I can say that, in some strange and possibly sick way, I felt more comfortable with myself in the "hot zone." It was as if I saw my own torment as a calling to do more. I felt my experience in Bosnia could shed some light for other soldiers in Kosovo. More importantly, I wanted to be and feel useful.

With divorce looming in my near future, I needed something to keep my mind occupied. The thoughts of having left my son in the same situation of not having his father raise him was killing me slowly. Telling myself over and over that I would not be like my own biological father didn't help at all. I felt I needed something that could occupy my thoughts entirely in order to stifle my feelings of being a failure. So I engulfed myself with work, training, and with my goal to head back to Kosovo.

My desire to return to Kosovo was met with only one option of going to a unit in Germany that might be getting deployed. The actual deployment was supposedly being scheduled for late 2000. I jumped on the opportunity without even thinking about it. In the end, I think the reenlistment sergeant was just trying to meet a quota, because I ended up going to a military intelligence unit that did not deploy to Bosnia or Kosovo.

The unit was the Sixty-Sixth Military Intelligence Regiment, and it was separated between two bases. The main body of the unit was located in Darmstadt, Germany, and the company that I was assigned to was located in Bad Aibling, Germany; it was Charlie Company.

Upon my arrival in Darmstadt, I was immediately notified that the chances of me deploying were slim to none. However, there was an open slot for me in Charlie Company that needed to be filled. Supposedly, the position had been offered to other logistics sergeants, but all had declined because the base was "away" from everything. Bad Aibling, Germany is located about thirty miles southeast of Munich, Germany, in southern Bavaria. The area itself is absolutely breathtaking, and I truly have no idea why anyone would turn down an assignment to this base aside from them not knowing any better. The base itself was generally thought to be an eavesdropping station allegedly connected to the Echelon system; a system that was believed to intercept global communications. During my time there, I even heard Dan Rather, the former *CBS News* anchor, refer to the base as a spy station.

When I arrived at the station, I found the place to be peaceful and welcoming. The unit itself was not something that I was accustomed to. Having supported a mechanized infantry unit for the past six years, I experienced a form of culture shock with my new duty assignment of supporting a military intelligence unit. For one, the operational tempo was 24-7, and the unit itself was far more tranquil than what I was used to. I was used to all the belligerent language, yelling, and chaotic pace that are commonplace in a rapid deployment unit and even more so in a combat infantry unit. The soldiers of Charlie Company were just as shocked with me. My harsh way in addressing matters was not something they were used to. They couldn't tell if I was serious and was, in fact, a hard-ass or if my personality was simply that of an asshole. My chain of command was shocked as well. They were not used to having someone with a "tell it like it is" attitude. The first couple of months there were a bit rough on everyone involved.

It was quickly determined that I needed far more collateral duties in order to keep busy. The motor pool of my new unit only had seventeen military vehicles and six civilian vehicles. I was used to dealing with a unit of over five hundred vehicles. My old shop alone had a total of seven vehicles, and that was just for our office. Granted, I was accustomed to supporting an entire battalion instead of just one company. Needless to say, my logistics job at Bad Aibling was easy when compared to that of Fort Hood, Texas, and thus needed more duties to keep me occupied.

One of those additional duties was that of being the barracks sergeant. With this duty, I mainly had to ensure that soldiers were living in suitable barracks and that their health and welfare were never placed at risk due to structural issues and cleanliness. The cleanliness clause was what some soldiers did not care for and thus made my job somewhat interesting. The only reason I could actually go into a soldier's room was to conduct health and welfare checks. When I first took over this particular assignment, I would only conduct the checks once every two weeks, but that had to change after our company first sergeant and I began to see that some of our soldiers were living in less-than-healthy conditions. So with the first sergeant's approval, I began conducting the health and welfare checks once a week. I would address issues with the individual soldiers and made sure they understood the deficiencies had to be taken care of within twenty-four hours. The beauty of human nature is that you will always have individuals that will push the envelope as far as they can when it comes to following rules or guidelines. This was the fun part, of course; at least, for me it was.

The main problem originally was that the soldiers of Bad Aibling would forget that I had spent the past six years with a combat infantry unit. I was not as easygoing or as politically correct as the other NCOs they had dealt with in the past were. This minor oversight ultimately led to them getting a whole bunch of ass chewings when there truly was no need for them. All they had to do was maintain the barracks clean. Yet the simplest of tasks can sometimes be the most daunting ones for certain individuals. After a few weeks, it was made clear by the soldiers' actions that I was just not getting through to them and thus needed to incorporate drastic measures.

One of the great things about being a leader in the military is that you get the chance to get creative when dealing with soldiers. I thought it was time to utilize scare tactics with those knuckleheads to make them actually appreciate their living conditions. I had come from a unit where soldiers had to share rooms and didn't truly have much privacy. Bad Aibling soldiers had individual rooms.

First thing I had to do was gain approval and backing from my chain of command. I went to the first sergeant's office one day and discussed all the infractions and deficiencies that had been addressed plenty of times with the soldiers. When I was asked what I had in mind to do, I shared my idea of using a scare tactic and having all the soldiers kicked out of the barracks and made to set up their army-issued shelter halves outside. This meant that they had to pair up in order to complete a tent that only granted enough room for two individual to lie side by side and nothing else. Whatever things they wanted to take outside with them would have to be left outside the tents while they slept and then placed back inside whenever they reported for work. Since their items couldn't be properly secured while they were working, this meant they had to share guard duties and leave one or two soldiers behind guarding everything while everyone else was working.

I remember the first sergeant smiling away and could tell that he loved the idea.

"Sergeant Tinoco, nothing like this has ever been done here. A lot of people are going to cry about this ordeal. I'm also 100 percent sure that the company commander and I will be getting a lot of phone calls from squad leaders and platoon sergeants about this."

"I understand that, First Sergeant. But you know all too well that, when petty stuff is left unchecked, it tends to become something far more serious and tougher to deal with in the long run. This may seem like madness, but there is logic behind it. I'm sure the soldiers will finally see that we mean business and are done accepting excuses for not maintaining their barracks clean."

I want to say that this was when I actually began using the phrases "There's logic to my madness" and "There's a method to my madness." Looking back, one may not find logic or method to some of the stuff I did, but in my mind, there was.

"Well, Sergeant Tinoco, I really like the idea, and I truly want to see the whole situation unfold. It should be interesting to watch. I'll explain it to the commander and then let you know when you can execute your plan."

"Roger that, First Sergeant."

I stood up, shook his hand, and walked out. I swear he had a smile the whole time just contemplating the crazy plan I had, or maybe he was probably just imagining what the commander's reaction would be once he was briefed on the plan. I never got to hear what his reaction was, but the next day, the first sergeant called me at my office to inform me that it was okay to carry out my plans.

"When do you have planned to execute this craziness?"

"Well, First Sergeant, I was thinking of Friday morning and allow it to drag into the evening for it to have maximum effect. Soldiers love their weekends, and something like this could really get their blood flowing."

"I like it, I really like it. Go for it, Sergeant Tinoco. Just remember that many squad leaders and platoon sergeants are going to raise hell about this. The commander and I decided to just keep the plan between the three of us, also for maximum effect. So if the other NCOs come to talk to you, just send them to me."

"Roger that, First Sergeant, Friday morning it is then."

The following couple of days, I conducted two more health and welfare inspections and found several deficiencies. I addressed those shortcomings just as I always had. Nothing changed in my demeanor; I was calm and collective the entire time. I was doing this with Friday in mind; I wanted that day to hit them hard and to truly shock them. Some of the things I addressed with the soldiers were taken care of, but some items were not. This was always the case, and it needed to change.

Friday morning, I conducted another inspection immediately at 8:00

a.m., and once again, most of the deficiencies that were constantly being addressed were still not up to par. I quickly went over to my office and began calling every platoon sergeant in the company and asking them to send me the soldiers who lived in the barracks. When asked for a reason, I would simply direct their questioning over to the first sergeant's office. For the most part, once I directed them to Top (nickname used for any company first sergeant), they wouldn't even bother calling his office and just send me the soldiers. I asked that the soldiers report to their barracks and wait for me in the break room.

Once all the soldiers were present, I stormed into the break room and allowed the madness to begin.

"I want every fucking soldier in here to pack up your duffel bags with your shelter halves and any sanitary items you deem necessary for the next week!"

All I got were blanked stares. They all sat or stood in place, trying to decipher the words I was yelling at them.

"I say again, I want all of you in here to go to your fucking nasty-ass rooms and pack up your shelter halves, along with clothes, your sleeping bags, and any sanitary items you might need for the next week! From this point on, these barracks are now closed and off-limits! The only areas that can be used are the showers and the restrooms!"

I could see the disbelief in their eyes and expressions as the words were slowly beginning to sink in.

"Move your fucking asses! I expect you outside with all your shit in a formation in ten minutes!"

I began walking out of the room, and that was when the silence broke. A bunch of the soldiers began crying out loud that I couldn't do this or that this shit was messed up. Several soldiers came over to me and asked if I was serious. Damn right, I was serious, and just like with their squad leaders and platoon sergeants, the moment I challenged them to go see Top to see if I meant business or not, they did as instructed.

I must say that it took everything in me to not smile as I walked away from them all, listening to all the commotion, doors slamming, wall-lockers being flung open, cursing, and whining. As I was making my way out of the building, Top was by the hallway, waiting for me.

"Some platoon sergeants have already called. I've told them they must adhere to everything you say and not to expect their soldiers back at work anytime soon."

"Thanks, Top, the soldiers have ten minutes to form up outside. If they're not all there, the games will truly begin."

"Okay, Sergeant Tinoco. Should I close my window?"

"You can, but you're still going to hear me."

He smiled and walked back toward his office.

Ten minutes passed, and I was outside, waiting on everyone to form up. I could still hear commotion from the barracks as soldiers were still trying to get all their things. Some of them had made it in time. I stood there in front of them, looking at their disheveled duffel bags with stuff protruding from them due to the short time they had been given. Although they had met my timeline for the formation, everyone was going to pay the price. I gave the few soldiers in formation a look of disappointment and then looked at my watch; two more minutes had passed.

"If your fellow soldiers are not here in the next fifteen seconds, I'm going to smoke the shit out of you until they do get here!"

The soldiers in formation began yelling out to their partners, "Hurry the fuck up! You're late! Move faster!"

Fifteen seconds passed; I assumed the position of attention and addressed the group.

"Group, attention! Half-right, face! Front-leaning-rest position, move!"

Once everyone was in the proper push-up position, I broke away from my spot and began pacing in front of the formation as I initiated the slow-paced rhythm of doing push-ups.

"Down."

Everyone went down and assumed the low end of the push-up position. I waited a few seconds to ensure their muscles were engaged.

"Up."

As everyone snapped to the start position, more of the soldiers trailed toward the formation.

"Form up along with your buddies and assume the push-up position! We are going to do this until everyone gets down here, and then we are going to continue pushing until I get tired!" Beauty of it all was that I wasn't pushing, so of course this messed with their minds even more because I would never get tired.

"Down."

This time, I allowed a few more seconds to pass. "Up."

"Some of your buddies are still not down here! I guess they don't mind you all doing push-ups for them!"

A few more soldiers trailed in, and they dropped their bags quickly to join their buddies. I proceeded with a fast pace of my commands so that they could get a good set of push-ups done. They must have done about fifty push-ups as more and more soldiers made it to formation and joined in. Once I saw that their arms had begun to shake, I stopped the exercise and called them to the position of attention. I addressed all the ongoing deficiencies that seemed to never get fixed even though I had already discussed those issues on numerous occasions in the past. I told them all that, since they couldn't keep their barracks clean, they were now going to be living out of their tents.

"You all have twenty minutes to figure out who your tent partner is going to be and then set up your tents in an organized fashion! Your partner will be of the same gender! Once everything is set up properly, I will assign your guard duties for today and this weekend! Aside from the restrooms and showers, your barracks are off-limits! I will be collecting your room keys shortly!"

Everyone just stood there in disbelief, trying to maintain the position of attention since they had just gotten smoked with push-ups. I could see the anger and the shock in their eyes.

"On the command of 'Fall out,' you will all get together and do as instructed. Remember, you have twenty minutes to get this done!"

I once again assumed the position of attention and made sure I locked eyes with everyone in the group. "Fall out!"

Everybody scrambled toward one another, grabbing their duffel bags, and quickly partnered up with each other. They were starting to get the idea. I decided to step away momentarily just to see if they would begin to bicker among themselves. Sure enough, the moment I stepped away, the bickering and whining began.

I listened to them as they all began to reproach the few known culprits who were always in violation of the cleaning duties or assignments. This was exactly what I wanted. I wanted the group to apply pressure on those soldiers who were not doing what they were supposed to. Taking their weekend away along with the comfort and privacy of their own rooms was going to either make them come together as one and not accept anything less than 100 percent participation in the maintaining of the barracks, or it was going to divide the group completely. I was shooting for the unification and their assertive resolution to finally do what was being demanded of them all. Otherwise, it was going to be mass punishment every single time someone failed inspection. It was in their best interest to unite, and from what I was listening to, it seemed that things were headed in that direction.

Twenty minutes were up.

I walked over to the front of the group, stood at the position of attention, and scanned over the soldiers still working on their tents.

"Group, attention!"

Everybody stopped what they were doing and assumed the position of attention.

"I must not be making myself clear! I thought I gave you twenty minutes to complete this task, and yet here we are with a bunch of unfinished and unsecured tents! Well, that's okay! I have something that might motivate you!"

I could see the panic in their eyes as they sighed and waited for the next command.

"Front-leaning-rest position, move!"

Everyone snapped into the push-up position, and I began a fast-paced count again. I keep them pushing until half the group began to collapse and was unable to continue.

"Oh hell! What the fuck is going on here? Some of you don't want to do push-ups anymore! That's okay too! Let's switch it up! On your backs!"

They all collapsed on the ground and painfully rolled over onto their backs.

"Flutter kicks on my count! Ready! Begin! One, two, three! One, two, three!"

Every time I reached the count of three, the soldiers yelled out a count of one and continued the count until they once again reached the point of exhaustion. I could hear their grunting and gasping as they tried to continue with the exercise.

"Okay, let's get ready for some front-back-go routine! You all know the drill! Once again, we're going to keep on doing this until you all make a believer out of me!"

More painful grunting from the entire group. "Front!"

Everyone assumed the push-up position and began to knock some out.

"Back!" Everyone turned over to the flutter-kick position and started to do the exercise.

"Go!"

Everyone stood up and began to run in place. I did this drill with them for about ten minutes before deciding to give them a break.

"Position of attention, move!"

Everyone tried their best to assume the position of attention. I could tell they were exhausted and barely able to stand straight.

"All right! You now have ten minutes to get your tents up, secured, and all your items inside them! Everything better be in an organized manner and in uniformity! If one tent setup looks different, may God help you all! Fall out!"

Once again, everyone rushed as best they could toward their respective tents, and some of the soldiers began hollering how to have their things set up inside or outside them. This was done so that they could all be uniformed identically. And still, the bickering continued as some of the soldiers continued to scold those few who were known to always fail the health and welfare inspections. Their teamwork was actually becoming more organized. They were becoming one team; at least for the task at hand.

Ten minutes passed.

I walked toward the group again. I could see that, for the most part, everyone was done with their tent. There were two soldiers still trying to organize their duffel bags in the manner that mirrored everyone else. I purposely called the group to attention right away before the soldiers could finish. After scolding them some more for still not having everything done as directed, I had them do more exercises. I smoked them for about another fifteen minutes without stopping. All the soldiers were collapsing and having a difficult time continuing with the exercises. After stopping the smoke session and calling them to attention once more, I gave them an additional five minutes to complete the task. After those five minutes were up, everything was set up as it should. I addressed the entire group and told them about their failure to comply with the demands of a health and welfare inspection. I told them that I was going to keep them outside for one week as punishment. Their weekend was shot as far as they knew. I had shattered their plans. Prior to calling it a day, I gave them one last task. They were to go into their barracks again and ensure that every common area was clean. They were given thirty minutes to complete the task.

During those thirty minutes, some of their squad leaders and platoon sergeants had made their way to my location. They had already addressed their disapproval of my actions to the first sergeant and the company commander. In order to maintain the illusion of actual punishment, these sergeants were not told the truth. They were pissed, to say the least. Several of them actually came over to me and asked me who the hell I thought I was. I was professional and told them someone had to finally remind the soldiers that they were,s in fact, soldiers. This meant they had to follow all policies, directives, and orders given to them. I offered them to take over my duties as the barracks sergeant, and none of them took me up on it. So they disagreed with my tactics but wouldn't take over to try something different.

Before the thirty minutes were up, all the soldiers were back in formation waiting on me to address them. I had them stand at ease while I took the floor leaders with me to inspect all the areas. I didn't find a single infraction. Afterward, I addressed the entire formation and informed them of their need for guards to stand watch over all their tents and belongings. The rest could go back to their respective shops and finish out their duty day. I informed them that we would have another formation at the end of the day along with three other formations on Saturday and Sunday. They were no longer giving me that blank stare of disbelief. The message had sunk in.

After I had them all fall out and assume their duties, I went back to the first sergeant's office. Both he and the commander briefed me on all the phone calls they had received from the affected platoons and how they had backed me up on the measures I had taken. I, in turn, advised them that I would hold two more formations at the end of the duty day, not one, as I had told the soldiers. I explained to them that the second formation would be held two hours after the close-of-business formation. My intent was to allow the soldiers time to actually believe their weekend was completely shot. That time would also grant them the opportunity to discuss their own shortcomings and come to an agreement of doing what's expected every single time moving forward. The commander and first sergeant were pleased with the idea and asked me to simply notify them once the final formation had taken place.

At the end of the day, we had our formation, and I informed the soldiers of their responsibilities for the weekend. I reminded them once again how the barracks were off-limits except the restrooms and showers. I collected all their room keys and had the floor leaders follow me once again as I made sure that all the rooms were locked. In closing, I told them that to make sure they were doing everything they were instructed. I would hold surprise formations periodically throughout the night and the weekend. This last statement is what broke their hearts, I think. I could see their hopes dwindle and shatter as the reality of it all finally sank in.

Two hours later, I had a surprise formation. Everyone was present, and when asked if they had learned anything that day, they all sounded off with a thunderous "Yes, Sergeant!" That was when I finally cautioned them of it being their final warning. They were to do what was expected of them, or they would be living outside. When I dismissed them from formation, they all just stood there. They weren't sure if I was serious about releasing them back to their rooms. I walked through the ranks, returning their room keys, and assured them that I was serious. I just asked them to never forget that day, and more importantly, I asked them to remember that I had the backing of our chain of command. They passed every single health and welfare inspection after that, and I never even had issues with new soldiers arriving; the soldiers made sure that everyone was aware of the consequences, and they held one another accountable.

The second duty that I was given was that of being the partnership NCO for the German-American Partnership Unit. This program unites American and German soldiers for various events that are set up to build camaraderie among the soldiers. Those events include qualifying with each other's service weapons, sports, Honor Guard ceremonies, hiking various mountains of Germany, and even social events as a form of community outreach.

When I was tasked with this assignment, participation was dismal. It is fair to state that the program was pretty much nonexistent. I was nervous at first. One, I felt I was being handed a sinking ship, and two, I had not learned the language yet.

My concerns faded once I got to know the two Germans who were in charge of the program on their side of the house. The officer in charge was Colonel Neuser, and the noncommissioned officer was Oberstabsfeldwebel (leading staff field usher) Dax. The great thing about them is that they spoke perfect English. They quickly gave me the history on the program's nineteen-year existence and their plans for improving it. We hit it off well, and once I met the other German soldiers, I was hooked. It was a great bunch of men.

This group of soldiers made my job fairly easy. They all enjoyed training our soldiers on the effective use of their German weapons and passing on what knowledge they had about the history of the surrounding area of Bad Aibling. The greatest thing is that they expected nothing in return. They had volunteered to participate in the program and were determined to make it a great experience for everyone involved. Their professionalism and graciousness made me want to do the same for them. I quickly utilized all the resources I had at my disposal as the motor pool sergeant to be able to provide transportation for as many soldiers as possible.

The great thing about my shop is that I had quick access to the German motor pool personnel and could easily and readily request buses for larger groups. I also had to do business with the bases located in Darmstadt, Stuttgart, Frankfurt, Heidelberg, and Mainz; this afforded me the opportunity to reach out to as many soldiers as possible and grant them the chance to participate in the program. Every soldier that came over to Bad Aibling to participate in the program left with a feeling of great accomplishment. Most were after the German proficiency marksmanship badge, the Schutzenschnur.

To earn the badge, a soldier must be able to qualify with three German weapons: the G36 rifle, the P8 pistol, and the MG3 machine gun. The badges are awarded in bronze, silver, and gold, depending on the score qualification that is achieved. Our German counterparts would train our soldiers on the weapons and then coach them throughout their attempt to qualify. They were great coaches. A few of them could not speak English, and most of our soldiers, myself included, only knew how to order a beer in German. This, of course, created a language barrier, which we all learned to overcome through the effective use of hand signals and loud voice tones. Funny how we always revert to using louder tones when trying to convey a message to a foreigner. This ordeal only added to the enjoyment of the experience. It was hilarious. We were training them in the English language, and they were training us in the German language. Neither of us understood what the other was saying verbally, but we all somehow understood all the hand signals and nonverbal cues very clearly. Everything was clear as mud, but we made the most of it and somehow were very successful.

The German soldiers, in turn, would be trained and qualified with our M16 rifle. Granted, our qualification badge was nothing to look at when compared to the Schutzenschnur, but our German friends didn't care about that at all. They wanted the opportunity to learn about and shoot our M16s.

Another key player in all this was my good friend Chris. He always helped me out with all the events and was also one of the firearms instructors at the range. Like me, he knew how to order a beer in German and had to revert to hand signals and hands-on instructions at the range. We made a pretty good team, chaotic but good. Chris had also deployed to Bosnia and had been involved in a few difficult situations. He used to work directly for the commanding general of the

United States Army Europe (USAEUR), General Eric K. Shinseki. He too was part of the support element and handled all of Charlie Company's administrative functions. He was sort of the human resources department for the company. There wasn't a partnership function that Chris was not involved in.

After each event, we would all gather at a local restaurant for dinner and drinks. This was always the case, and we used this particular setting every time to give the soldiers from both countries the opportunity to coalesce and learn from each other. It was always a great time, and the amazing German beer was always on hand to help us out with the language barrier that existed between us. Fortunately, as time went by, a few of us were able to learn the German language better, and more of the German soldiers were able to learn the English language as well. It's safe to say that whatever inhibitions we had regarding our abilities to speak and understand each other's language were washed away fairly quickly with the help of German beer and schnapps. Every event started out the same way when it came to mingling at the local restaurants. Chris and I made sure that all the tables had a mixture of American and German soldiers and the first ten minutes or so were always quiet. But once those beers and shots of schnapps kicked in, we couldn't stop the soldiers from talking to one another in their best broken English or German. It was an interesting thing to see unfold before us, and they were truly great times.

With time, our participation numbers grew extensively. I had to coordinate with the German motor pool and get bus drivers for every event. Some of our events actually forced me to utilize up to three commercial buses because so many soldiers were participating. I was happy to accommodate as many soldiers as possible, and the German leadership was ecstatic that the program was doing so well.

My favorite event of the partnership was the mountain training event that we would do only once a year. We would go hiking up the mountains in Brannenburg, Germany. There is a cottage halfway up the highest summit, the Wendelstein, which is a 6,030-foot-high mountain. This mountain is part of the Bavarian Alps of Southern Germany. The cottage itself was built during WWII and completed in 1945. It is utilized by the German armed forces for mountain training, especially those units belonging to the German Mountaineer Brigade.

We would spend two days and two nights at the cottage. Once we hiked up to it, we would use it as our starting point the next two days. Soldiers were taken up to five different summits during the two-day training: Lacherspitz, Wendelstein, Soinwand, Kesselwand, and Wildalpjoch. None of us ever saw it as training though. The scenery up there was breathtaking. Our German counterparts would take along their own military cooks and a few instruments for some polka music at the end of each day. Keep in mind, one can't truly listen to German polka music without some German beer and schnapps. Chris and I had become very good friends with some of the German soldiers. Neuser, Dieter, Faist, Lutz, Miedl, and Kleinmeier are just a few of the great men who gave so much of themselves to make these events work to everyone's benefit.

Faist was a true Mountaineer Brigade soldier, and he took those hikes very seriously. Of the entire partnership unit, he was the only soldier to have ever earned the famous edelweiss badge and patch for wear on his uniform. This badge is designed to resemble the edelweiss flower, which grows on the highest points of the Alps. Germans believe that specially trained mountain troops are what influence the outcome of any major military campaign that is surrounded by mountains. After having gone through the partnership unit's version of mountain training two years in a roll, I got the courage to ask Faist what it would take for me to earn the edelweiss badge. I remember Faist looking around at his partners and having a huge grin on his face before responding to my question in his most broken English.

"The training is very tough!"

"Can you train me?"

He actually laughed out loud at my comment while I just sat there wondering why this man wouldn't think it possible for me to earn such a prestigious award. When he finally saw that my composure hadn't changed, he too became very serious.

"Are you sure, Sergio?"

"Yes. I would like to earn your respect."

"You already have my respect. No need for anything else to be done."

"Wrong. I would like for you to see that I can do this, but with one condition."

"What is condition?"

"When I do earn your respect as a Mountaineer soldier, I would like for you to pin the edelweiss on me, nobody else."

By this time, Dieter, Neuser, Lutz, and a few other German soldiers had weighed in on our conversation and were all anxious to see if Faist would accept me as his *Praktikant* , "trainee" or "pupil." Faist considered the fact that I had already earned the German Sports Badge (Deutsches Sportabzeichen), which is a decoration of the German Olympic Sports Federation for qualifying in five different events that test a soldier's physical ability, strength, and endurance. Those five events are a two-hundred-meter swim; a long jump, which measures a person's jumping power; a thousand-meter run, and a five-hundred-meter bicycling event, to measure speed; a shot-put event and another hundred-meter swim to indicate a person's physical strength; and lastly, the measurement of one's endurance was done by way of a twenty-three-mile triathlon.

I have never been a good swimmer, and I have always hated to run, yet I was able to push through my fear of deep water and my hatred of running to be able to earn this award. If asked to complete these disciplines now, I would probably laugh.

I could tell that Faist was hesitant about taking me on as a pupil. Our work schedules were our greatest obstacle, but I swore to make myself available whenever he requested for whatever training I had to go through. He talked it over with Colonel Neuser for a few moments and then gave me his answer. He would train me. I was overjoyed, but I did ask him for one last thing. I asked to be treated as a new German soldier who had joined the ranks of the Mountaineer Brigade. I didn't want special treatment with regard to the training regimen. Faist smiled, shook my hand, and swore that he would train me hard; afterward, he wished me luck. All of us there were ecstatic. The German soldiers couldn't believe this was taking place. It was something completely unexpected and something that had not been asked of them throughout their years of military service.

The training was scheduled to last three months. This was due in part to our actual work schedules and other partnership events that were already on our calendar, and we had agreed that my individual training would not interfere with the partnership program in any way. Three months prior to my last mountain training event in Brannenburg, Faist began coaching me on mountain survival and pushing me even harder on my physical strength, endurance, and stamina. I was going to need it in order to survive the hike of eight different summits in two days. At the end of the three months, Faist, Dieter, and Colonel Neuser came over to Bad Aibling Station to have dinner and drinks with me. Because of Faist's broken English and my broken German, Dieter was our middleman and helped us out whenever something was not understood between us. Faist asked me how I felt and if I believed I was ready. I remember pausing and thinking about my response prior to answering the questions. Not something I was known for doing.

"Yes, I think I'm ready, and I feel great, actually."

Faist looked at me and then reached across the dining table. "No, not what was asked."

I paused again, contemplated his questions. "Ja, Ich glaube." Yes, I believe.

I had to think of my translation. Was it correct? "Ja, Ich bin bereit. Yes, I'm ready.

I paused again and waited for Faist to respond. The seconds in between seemed to drag, as if someone had requested a moment of silence and everyone at the table had agreed to it.

I turned over toward the Colonel and Dieter to see if maybe I could get a hint from them that my German statement was wrong. They just nodded back toward Faist.

As I looked at Faist again; his grin began to widen and slowly became a huge smile. He stood up and reached for my shoulders.

"I believe this too, Sergio! You must believe!"

And at that, we all stood up gleaming with excitement. Faist and I were both congratulated by the Colonel and Dieter. Together, we had accomplished a great first step toward my earning the famous edelweiss. After a few moments of cheer and ordering more drinks to celebrate, we continued our dinner and discussed the date for my actual certification training. It was set for one month before our upcoming mountain training partnership event. I was given a list of items to pack for my certification and told to hydrate well the entire week prior. No beer, I was told. After our dinner, the three of them left the station, and all wished me the best of luck. I was experiencing an immense mixture of excitement, relief, gratitude, and astonishment all at once. I couldn't believe this was actually happening.

Two days after my meeting with Faist, the colonel, and Dieter, I got a visitor at my office in the motor pool. It was a tall individual in uniform. I quickly scanned over his BDU to catch a name and rank, but I couldn't find a name tag on him or any rank insignia.

"Sergeant Tinoco?"

"Yes."

"Hello, I'm Sergeant Major Breasse. Alpha 1-10, Special Forces, out of Stuttgart, Germany."

His introduction caught me off guard. Special Forces? "Hello, Sgt. Major. How can I help you?"

"I talked to your company commander, and he informed me that you were the man to see with regards to helping out my guys with some support for a mountain training exercise they're starting in a few weeks."

"Sure thing, Sergeant Major. Anything you guys need."

"Good to hear that, Sergeant. I'll have one of my men contact you prior to the training so that you guys can hash out all the specifics and logistics."

"Roger-that, Sergeant Major." It turned out that the actual days of their training were the same days I was supposed to go through the mountaineer training with Faist.

Duty first.

In any case, it turned out to be a great endeavor. I was able to go out and support the Special Forces unit during their training. The unit was pretty awesome. The guys even allowed me to partake in some of their survival training on one of the summits that had to be reached. My German friends understood that this was my job and there was no way I could tell a group of soldiers, especially the Green Beret, that I couldn't support them. At that time, I figured that I would have another opportunity to earn the edelweiss badge. Unfortunately, due to the German Mountaineer Brigade actually undergoing their own training, I never got a chance.

When the time came for me to partake in my last mountain training exercise with the partnership unit, Faist and a few of the other German soldiers hiked along with me. For two days, I talked to them about what a great time I'd had while running the program. This caught them off guard a bit since they didn't know that it would be my last mountain training exercise with them. I was on my last year in Germany and had to start looking for another American soldier to take my place in running the program. Our conversations that weekend were joyful for the most part. We reminisced on all the great times we had had with the program. We tried our best to not turn the talking points into a melancholic state of mind. Yet after every hike up the designated summits, drinks were poured once we made our way back to the cottage—cheerful music, great food, great company, and the ever-tasteful German beer. Emotions always tend to get the best of people once the drinks begin to flow. It was no different for my German friends and me.

On our last evening there, Faist presented me with his black beret. The man had a big grin on his face and was doing his best to express himself in English. Pinned on the beret was an edelweiss badge. It was such a heartfelt honor for me. Everyone cheered and brought their beer glasses together in toasts and approval of the tremendous sign of respect that Faist had just bestowed upon me. I was speechless, choking with emotion as this man had truly believed in me and in my ability to have been able to survive the mountaineer training. I thanked him and gave him a great, big bear hug. I held on to that beret for the rest of the night. I didn't even wear it, because I couldn't stop admiring the edelweiss on it. I was in such disbelief.

A few months later, my German friends would surprise me once again by awarding me with the German Badge of Honor in Bronze, the highest award they themselves could earn for being in the Reservisten der Bundeswehr, German Army Reserves. To say that I was overwhelmed and speechless is an understatement. It is my understanding that

Colonel Neuser and Dieter were instrumental in the push for the medal to be awarded to me. It is a medal that has taken me years to even talk about. I never believed that I had done anything that could be considered outside the norm. I was a soldier just as they were. I did what needed to be done and nothing more.

Colonel Neuser and Dieter both pulled me to the side after the award presentation. They told me they were proud of the work we had done together. To them, that particular award presentation was also a first. Looking back now, fourteen years later, I still can't believe I was fortunate enough to have ever earned their respect. That ceremony was supposed to be a joyful one, but we all knew that my time with them was coming to an end. The thought of no longer being able to work with them turned it into a somber occasion. It was a truly humbling experience.

Cabin used during the Partnership Unit's mountain training
weekends in the mountains of Brannenburg, Germany

Taking a break at one of the mountain tops in Brannenburg, Germany

On my way up toward those mountains in the background

9/11

. . . .

It was midafternoon on September 11, 2001. Time in Germany is about seven hours ahead of the East Coast time in the United States. I was working on some maintenance reports for the motor pool in my office when the phone rang. It was my company commander.

"Sergeant Tinoco, how long will it take you to activate the Quick Reaction Force (QRF) and shut down this base?"

Still not knowing what for.

"Should only take me about an hour, Sir."

"Okay. The United States is under attack. I'll give you thirty minutes to shut this place down and then report to our conference room for a meeting."

"Roger that, Sir."

Without hesitating, I began calling all the soldiers of the QRF. The message was simple, "Drop what you're doing, gear up, draw your weapons, and link up with me in front of the company headquarters." I closed the message by telling them all with a stern voice, "This is not a fucking drill!" I needed them to know that every second was crucial.

After notifying the entire team, I called the Military Police office and coordinated our efforts with them so that neither team spent time doing something that had already been done by the other. I closed the shop up and quickly made my way to the company headquarters. Half of the team was already there; the other half made it to our rally point a minute or two later. The company executive officer (XO), First Lieutenant (LT) Tingley, and I had a good team of soldiers for the QRF. I quickly gave them all the same statement that had been given to me: that the United States was under attack. I broke them into four teams and gave each team a set of instructions and responsibilities.

Fifteen minutes had already passed.

"We have less than fifteen minutes to shut this place down and ensure everyone in here is secure! Nobody comes into this base without our say-so! Nobody leaves this base without our say-so! I will be standing by the radio and waiting for you all to report back to me and let me know that your areas are secure! Any questions?"

"No, Sergeant!"

"Move your asses, let's go, let's go, let's go!"

The entire team did everything they had been trained for. The LT and I had drilled them to death in preparation for any emergency response the base might require of us should the need ever arise. The fact that the base was considered a spy base of sorts, we had to prepare for anything and everything. Yet it's safe to say that the LT and I had never imagined needing the QRF for something like what was taking place on that day.

About twelve minutes later, all three teams reported their specific areas secure. One team would remain at the main gate along with the MPs, two teams would patrol inside the base, and the remaining two teams would patrol outside the wire.

The MPs were already reporting two media crew members outside the main gate. They were to be kept outside the base until further notice and could not be allowed to point their cameras into the compound at all.

I made my way into the conference room and gave the LT a status update for the company commander. The television inside the room was on the Armed Forces Network (AFN) channel. This was when I first saw the images of the airplanes flying into the World Trade Center Towers. The other platoon sergeants and I just stood there at first, shocked by what we were seeing. It took us all a few moments before we actually took our seats at the table and continued watching the news as we waited for our company commander. Nothing any of us there had done throughout our military careers could have prepared us for what we were watching unfold in the news. None of us could have ever imagined something like that happening. You could have heard a pin drop in that room. The silence among us was deafening.

When the company commander walked in, the television was muted, and the meeting began. The LT and I were in charge of the QRF, so we already had our marching orders with regard to the security of the base and everyone inside it. A team of twelve soldiers was not going to be sufficient enough to run security operations twenty-four hours a day. More soldiers would be tasked out to us. A command post would be set up for the operation. It would be the one-stop shop for all base security matters. Roving patrols would be needed, gate guards to help the MPs with the inspection of all vehicles and personnel going into and out of the base.

After our meeting, I quickly checked in on the QRF and made sure everyone was okay. I gave them the news of having to stay on duty until we were all relieved the next morning. It was going to be a very long night for us, and I wanted to make sure the soldiers were well informed of the situation.

I then went back to my office and began calling the soldiers' spouses and inform them of the situation as well. I wanted to place them at ease and let them know that they probably wouldn't see their husbands until the following day. I asked them to be patient and supportive of their husbands. Lastly, I asked them to expect their husbands to have a very grueling schedule for the next couple of weeks, if not months.

The first three or four days were extremely hectic for us. Our base had been pinpointed by a national news program as the "spy base responsible for intercepting all communications between Al Qaeda." The assholes on the news even placed a map of Germany and pointed out our exact location during the newscast. Bad Aibling Station had just been made a target on national television to the entire world. Within hours of that newscast, media swarmed toward the base and did their best to set up camp in the surrounding area. Everything had to be reported to our commander, who in turn would report everything up the chain. Any media attempt to breach our security was dealt with swiftly. Everyone involved was committed to the mission at hand. All soldiers involved in the security operations still had to perform their regular duties. I still had to run the motor pool, take care of the barracks, run the partnership unit, and I had picked up the additional duties of a supply sergeant because our assigned staff sergeant had already reported to his next duty station.

The hour or so that I had spent in that first initial meeting with our company commander was probably the only time I had seen the news. I do recall seeing bits and pieces of it during the first two weeks after the attacks, but I never truly sat down and became consumed by the images and new reports that were taking place. I didn't have the time to do so. So all the raw emotions of anger, hate, despair, and fear that millions of other people were feeling during that first year after the attacks were not known to me. One, I couldn't truly relate since I had only caught a glimpse of what had taken place, and that was through the AFN channel. All the conversations that were taking place stateside were not taking place around me. Everyone around me was focused on the task at hand, and none of us had the time to actually sit down and discuss the horrible ordeal our people in the States were going through.

If we weren't physically engaged doing something, we were busy documenting everything we were doing—act, report; act, report. We were in a constant whirlwind of performing security measures and then reporting those same measures up the chain of command. The first time I actually experienced some of those raw emotions was in 2009. I had taken a trip to New York City. During that trip, I walked into the 9/11 Museum and was overwhelmed with emotion when I began listening to all the radio chatter from the day of the attacks. Later on in 2011, I went through a similar experience while watching all the 9/11 specials that were airing on television. Some of the footage shown on those specials was all new to me. It felt as if I were going through that ordeal for the first time ever, even though it was ten years later. A wave of mixed emotions swept over me as I was glued to the television, watching every special that aired. I felt angry, I felt hopeless, and for some strange reason, I felt guilty. Why I felt guilty, I can't say; I don't know. Maybe it was guilt for not being here in the United States when it all happened. For not being a part of the melancholic state of being that millions of Americans went through during and after the attacks. To some extent, I felt ashamed somehow. Where was I? What was I doing? Why don't I remember these images protruding from my television screen?

Even now, fifteen years later, I can't explain what I was feeling or why I was feeling that way. I know where I was, and I know what I was doing, but I felt guilty for not grasping the depth of it all back in 2001.

Final Year in the Army

· · · · · · · · · · · · · · · · · · · ·

In the spring of 2002, the First Lieutenant Tingley and I began training a group of soldiers for a one-hundred-mile ruck march that takes place in Nijmegen, the Netherlands. The team had to remain together and walk twenty-five miles a day for four days. We each had to carry a rucksack weighing thirty pounds. This is an amazing event. Thousands of civilians and military groups from various countries join the event every year. The routes take you through several towns that had all been overtaken by Germany during WWII. During the march, one actually walks across two key bridges of Nijmegen that played an important role in Operation Market Garden.

Having done the march, wearing our army BDUs, we encountered a great number of people who were kids during WWII. They would be sitting or standing alongside the route of travel and would come up to us with flowers to shower us with hugs and kisses. This was done in appreciation for what our soldiers had done for them back during the great war . The city of Nijmegen was liberated by the Eighty-Second Airborne Division. Nobody in our team was even alive during the war, yet we were treated as though we had liberated the city.

Doing the twenty-five miles a day was tough. Most of us ended up with blisters and swollen feet. After the march, I couldn't wear my military boots for about a week because my feet were so swollen. It took us all a few days to be able to walk without limping. I remember the LT and I would walk alongside our formation from time to time during the march just so that we could share stories with our soldiers. We did so with the intention of getting their minds off the pain they were experiencing. We would sing cadence in order to encourage one another. Soldiers and civilians from the other participating countries would join in from time to time as a form of stimulation or inspiration to continue moving forward. The months we had actually spent training for this event did help and prepared us for it, but it was still very tough on all of us.

At the end of each day, First Sergeant Hodgkins would treat our feet and help mend whatever ailments we were having. After the medical treatments were administered, we would all make our way to a beer tent that was set up for everyone to unwind, relax, and continue to encourage one another for the next day's march. It was an amazing feat, and I am honored to have been a part of that team. This march takes place every year with close to or over fifty thousand participants.

Having received the edelweiss badge from Faist, awarded the German Badge of Honor, and successfully completed the one-hundred-mile march, I didn't think anything else could possibly top off these experiences while in Germany. I was wrong.

As a final trip before leaving the country and heading toward my final duty station, I was able to go on a trip to the beaches of Normandy. I have always been fascinated by history, and maybe due to my military career, I have grown to love and appreciate military history. Prior to embarking on this trip, I read up on the great invasion that would lead to the liberation of France and, ultimately, the surrender of Germany. I was amazed by everything I read. The way our elite military units actually swam to the beaches in order to get samples of sand to see if our equipment could make it on land. The constant back and forth of weather forecasting or predicting for our soldiers to have the best possible chance of success. Even learning of the political deals that were taking place behind the seams between the Allied commanders was interesting.

The trip itself was a humbling experience. Seeing what the Allied Forces had to face as they stormed toward Omaha Beach and Checkpoint Charlie was unbelievable. The various cemeteries lined up with the gravestones of our fallen heroes was overwhelmingly melancholic, to say the least.

The remainder of my time spent in Germany was full of going-away cookouts and parties with all my friends. I had trained and soldiered many of soldiers of Charlie Company throughout my three years there. I am proud to say that many of them became great friends of mine and I still keep in touch with some of them, thanks to the social media outlets that are available today. Leaving Germany was a very sad moment. I wish I could have stayed there at least until the base closed in 2004. Unfortunately, because I had chosen not to reenlist anymore, I was not allowed to finish my military career there.

My final duty station was Fort Riley, Kansas. I was once again assigned to a rapid deployment, mechanized infantry unit: Headquarters Company of the First Brigade, First Battalion, Sixteenth Infantry Regiment (HHC 1-16th). I was now part of the First Infantry Division, otherwise known as Big Red One.

When I arrived at Fort Riley, I had one plan in mind. Aside from taking care of all my out-processing from the army, I wanted to continue my college education and at least complete an associate's degree while also figuring out what type of job to look for once I exited the army.

It turned out that I had two major obstacles in my way. The battalion I was assigned to was scheduled to deploy to Iraq in early 2004. This became the leading factor of my issues throughout my final year of service. My company first sergeant did not want to authorize me to attend night classes because I had chosen not to reenlist with our deployment to Iraq approaching. According to the first sergeant, I needed to commit to the Big Red One and to the army in order for him to allow me to attend school.

When he first told me this, I was flabbergasted. This man had not even bothered to check and see if I had ever deployed or been in a hot zone throughout my career. He was actually talking to me as though I had just enlisted and had never done anything for the army. He was a stubborn old man who was not going to be convinced otherwise and would not sign the necessary paperwork for me to attend school. Needless to say, had I given in to his hard-headedness, I would have reenlisted and begun training with the rest of the unit for the upcoming deployment. I would still not have been allowed to attend school for my own professional growth and development. Soldiering was the only education I needed in his mind. Regardless of the fact that I was still committed to training my soldiers for the deployment, the first sergeant didn't care. He had made up his mind. Hell, he wouldn't even let me speak to the company commander about the situation.

I was left with no other choice than to write a congressional letter. I wrote to my congressman, informing him of the situation at hand and of my military background. In my letter, I also explained how, even if I was not allowed to attend school, I was still going to leave the army in less than a year. Even with our deployment to Iraq, my particular job title was not being kept from exiting the military. In essence, there was nothing that my first sergeant could do to keep me in the army.

A month or so later, my company commander called me into his office. He wanted to discuss the letter he had received from my congressman. I explained my situation to him and informed him that I had requested to speak with him numerous times but that the first sergeant wouldn't allow it. When asked if there was anything that could be done to convince me to reenlist, I simply said no. My mind was made up. Truth be told, my mind was made up while I was still in Germany. A couple of weeks later, I was in school.

The second obstacle I encountered was my battalion commander. This man had come up with a policy that, if we couldn't convince him that we had a good plan for employment after leaving the army, he wouldn't sign our documents to exit the service. Although he had good intentions and wanted soldiers to actually have a plan for life after the army, I took it as a slap in the face.

I was not a kid who needed to ask him for permission to leave the army.

My commitment was up, and that was all he needed to be concerned with. Why did I have to convince him that I had a good plan? Why the hell did it even matter? I once again had to meet with the first sergeant, the company commander, and even him, the battalion commander, to ask what would actually happen if he didn't like my plan. Was he going to force me to remain in the army? I was furious.

In hindsight, I think he really did have a soldier's best interest in mind. He had just worded his policy incorrectly, and he was under the pressures of keeping as many soldiers as possible for the upcoming deployment. At the end of it all, I was not forced to stay any longer than I had to. I was able to complete an associate's degree prior to exiting the military, and I was able to sign out of Fort Riley, Kansas, on October 2003.

Anger and Depression

. . . .

Throughout my time in Germany, I became an alcoholic. If I was not engaged working, I was drinking heavily. When I first got to Germany, I was having a difficult time sleeping and felt that I had to drink myself to sleep every night. This was due to experiencing two very strong emotions and not knowing how to counter them or deal with them. I couldn't stop thinking of the things I had encountered while deployed in Bosnia. I used to think that I would eventually stop having nightmares and stop thinking about the deployment altogether. I could never have been more wrong.

Unknown to all the soldiers around me, I was having a very tough time with depression and anger. When I say anger, I mean full-on rage. I didn't know what was happening to me, and I didn't know how to control these emotions that would just hit me when I least expected it. I would be fine one moment and then completely enraged or depressed the next. At first, I dealt with it as I would deal with most of my problems at the time; I would simply work myself to the point of exhaustion. I had to keep my mind occupied with something other than whatever feelings I was experiencing at the moment.

When that didn't seem to work, I began to drink heavily. It didn't help much that I actually relished German beer. With time, though, beer was not enough. I began drinking liquor: rum, whiskey, tequila, schnapps. Being in a military installation with a bunch of young soldiers, I had an endless supply of beer and liquor. I was known to just grab bottles of whiskey or tequila and chug them down as though they were water. A friend of mine couldn't place a beer, a shot, or a bottle of liquor in front of me because it would go down quick. I'd like to think that I hid most of my issues at bay from my friends and from work. Only they would be able to answer that question now. I've asked some of them on various occasions but fear that they haven't shared their true thoughts on the matter for fear of insult. If they only knew how much I regret ever exposing them to the nightmare I had become.

When the emotions began to overwhelm me to a point where I felt I had lost complete control, I chose to counter them against each other. What does that mean?

Well, whenever I felt overpowered by depression, I would think of anything that would make me mad. Unfortunately, that anger actually came in the heightened state of rage for me. The opposite could be said of my way for countering my rage. I would listen to sad music and reminisce on some of the saddest moments of my life. Things that I had no control of yet somehow still blamed myself for them. I can't explain why, but I can say that, at that time, I felt I needed it in order to gain some sense of control over my own emotions and thoughts.

Another way of coping with my anger was working out. I had given myself a routine of waking up every morning at four o'clock to go hit the gym and work out until about five forty-five. At 6:00 a.m., I would show up to our company formations and do physical training with my soldiers. The PT sessions would last until about eight o'clock in the morning. Most days, I would hit the gym again at lunchtime and then again at the end of the duty day.

That was a total of four workouts a day, Monday through Friday. My workouts on the weekends depended entirely on how wasted I had gotten on Friday night and Saturday night or if I had a German partnership event going on that had kept me from getting wasted the night prior. In any case, I would still get at least two workouts on Saturdays and Sundays.

I would work out every major muscle group, every single day. I had plenty of workouts to do so. This was all done with the intent of ending the day exhausted and being able to get a decent night's rest. I didn't want to have nightmares. I didn't want to spend my nights imagining the soldiers in Bosnia crying in front of me or telling me about their nightmares. I couldn't stop the visions of bodies falling apart in my hands. I couldn't stop seeing kids shooting at my team as we tried to rescue other kids. I hated what I was going through. I hated myself for struggling with those thoughts and not being able to control them.

Yet I would still receive letters from those soldiers telling me that they were grateful for everything I had done for them. Grateful for having been there in their time of need. This only added to my depression. Instead of feeling proud for the things I was reading or being told, I felt guilty for how I was coping with my own demons. For as fit and strong as I was back then, I only saw myself as a weak individual.

How could they possibly believe that they would follow me through hell if need be when I was falling apart inside? My biggest fear was ever letting any soldier down, and so I pushed myself every day to be the best that I could possibly be in front of them. This was a debilitating feat when I was feeling miserable inside. I felt I had to hide my innermost thoughts and fears from everyone so that I could still be there for them. I was struggling to coexist as two different persons. The person fighting his own affliction and the person the soldiers around me thought I was.

The one thing I could rely on to help me cope with my inner demons was the job itself. It might be that the job forced me to push through it all and not necessarily help. Once again, this can only be answered by those individuals who were around me during that time. People like Chris, Buford, Henage, Williams, Cartier, Chialda, Dula, and Mack, to name a few, are the ones who got to see me at my worst. Chris is probably the one I confided in more than I did in anyone else yet was the one person I ended up placing in the hospital after one of my moments of rage. In what was probably my darkest moment, I got completely wasted one night at a nightclub. From what I recall, I had accidentally bumped into a table and spilled everyone's drinks. I remember apologizing and paying for another round to make up for my drunken clumsiness, but the men at that table were Turkish. They were not fond of American soldiers, and they were not accepting my apology or the round of drinks I had bought them. So the fight began. I must have punched and fought off everyone around me, which in turn led to a much-bigger fight with other folks and more soldiers. We ended up shutting down the club that night, and even that wasn't enough. I was still angry at everything and everyone; Chris said something to me or bumped into me, and I just started swinging.

By the end of the night, Chris had ended up in the hospital, and I had damaged a bunch of vehicles in the parking lot. A few of the soldiers had rallied around me and somehow got me into a vehicle and took me back to the base. Once at the base and in the safety of my own room, I passed out. I didn't find out about Chris ending up in the hospital until the following morning. Guilt hit me hard once I was told that I had put Chris in the hospital. I had lost control, hit rock bottom. To make matters worse, when I went to go visit Chris in the hospital, he was reading the book *Band of Brothers*. We laugh about it now, but it really made me feel like the lowest piece of shit back then.

Chris and I had become the best of friends. There wasn't anything we wouldn't do for each other. We were like brothers. Yet none of that had mattered in my drunken state. The rage I felt within had blinded me and taken complete control. My chain of command had no recourse but to investigate the whole ordeal and seek punishment. I remember my lieutenant and Staff Sergeant Dula, my platoon sergeant, trying their best to minimize my punishment. Even Chris wouldn't tell the MPs that I had been the one to place him in the hospital. He kept telling the MPs and our chain of command that he couldn't remember who it was. I can never thank them enough for having the courage and even the will to speak on my behalf to the company commander and the rest of my chain. Needless to say, I was damaged, and I needed help. The things I had done that night could not go unpunished though. Aside from being stripped of my promotable status for staff sergeant, I was banned from the bar on post, I could not purchase any alcohol anywhere, and I had to attend Alcoholics Anonymous for a period that was to be determined by my company commander.

Yet it wasn't the punishment that forced me to wake the hell up. My punishment lasted for about four months. It was a struggle at first. I couldn't face anyone without feeling guilty and, worse, like a failure. No, I didn't truly wake up until the company commander called me into his office for a meeting. I remember that meeting as though it just took place yesterday.

The first sergeant had called me at my office and told me to report immediately to his office. I closed down the shop and went right away. After reporting to him, he told me to take a sit outside his office and wait for the commander to call me in. A few minutes passed before the commander opened his door and directed me inside.

"Have a seat, Sergeant."

As I sat down in front of his desk, he grabbed a military records jacket and showed it to me.

"Do you know what this is?"

"Yes, sir. It's someone's military record."

"Correction, Sergeant Tinoco, this is your military record. I called you in today so that we could discuss what's in it."

I was puzzled and wondered what for.

"I'm sure it's no secret, Sergeant, that I've had your platoon sergeant, the first sergeant, and even the company XO keep tabs on you for the past four months."

"No, sir. They've been on me pretty much every single day since my punishment began."

He dropped the military record directly in front of me.

"They all feel that you've learned your lesson and that I should lift the punishment imposed upon you."

I remained quiet.

"Go ahead and open your file, Sergeant."

I grabbed the file and opened it as ordered. I could see that several documents were not affixed to the file properly. As I paged through the loose documents, I saw my deployment orders from Fort Hood to Bosnia, various sets of orders for medals I had been awarded, the German awards, and lastly, the orders for the German Badge of Honor, which had been fought for by my dear German friends.

"Sergeant Tinoco, would you agree with me when I say that you have a drinking problem?"

I looked up at him; he was still standing. "Yes, Sir."

"I've made some calls and can only assume that Bosnia is the cause of your drinking. Am I correct in that?"

I didn't know what to say. I knew it was; I just couldn't or didn't want to say it out loud. How could I admit that my job or the work I had done was the cause of my drinking? It felt like such a copout.

"I don't know, sir."

He looked at me. I could only guess he was trying to determine if I was full of shit or truly couldn't face the reasoning behind my explosiveness.

"Okay, Sergeant Tinoco. Let me rephrase this matter for you." He paused in order to gather his thoughts. I waited.

"Sergeant Tinoco, do you want everything you've ever worked for and accomplished in the army to be diminished or possibly even lost because of your alcoholic issues? Or better yet, do you want this jacket and everything in it to not mean a damn thing to the army nor to anyone that knows you well because of your behavior?"

Of course I didn't want that. Why the hell would he even ask me that?

"No, sir!"

"Then I suggest you get your act together, Sergeant! A lot of soldiers look up to you! A lot of soldiers depend on you! Other NCOs and officers have tremendous respect for you! The German soldiers speak very highly of you all the time! Does any of this mean anything to you? Do the awards in this file mean anything to you at all?"

"Yes, sir!"

My voice cracked as I responded. Of course all that meant something to me. It was all I had. It meant everything to me.

He finally sat down and changed his demeanor. "If I lift your punishment, will I live to regret it?"

I couldn't answer. I couldn't even look at him. My eyes were fixed on my file and its contents. How could anyone ask if any of it meant anything to me? Is that what the soldiers were asking themselves whenever they saw me? Was I being seen as a failure? Had I truly gone off the deep end?

I lifted my head to face the commander as I began to tremble. I was trembling with fear and guilt. Had my greatest fear become true? Had I failed everyone around me? I could feel my body heating up as tears began to trail down my face. I locked eyes with my commander.

"No, sir! You will never regret this! This will never happen again!"

He looked at me as though trying to decipher the words I was saying.

We kept our eyes locked on each other for what felt like an eternity. My trembling became an uncontrollable shake. The commander finally broke contact, stood up, and walked around his desk toward me.

I stood up to face him.

"I believe you, Sergeant Tinoco, but I still want you to promise me something."

"What's that, sir?"

"Promise me that you'll never forget what's in that file. Promise me you'll think of that file every day."

"I promise, sir."

He shook my hand with a strong, firm grip and patted me on the shoulder.

"Okay. Your punishment ends today. Don't be quick to celebrate, and don't forget what you promised."

"Thank you, sir. I won't forget."

I was dismissed and made my way back to my office. It was a ten-minute walk back, yet it felt like it took me an hour. The entire way back, all I could think about was my military file. I had to change somehow. I wasn't sure how, but I had to. The past four months had been sort of an eye-opener. I didn't have to get drunk and wasted like I used to. I could control it. I could be just as disciplined off duty as I was on duty. For the remainder of my stay in Germany, I did venture to enjoy drinks with my friends; I just never drank again like I used to. I think the only time I had liquor again was at my farewell cookout, and it was nasty garlic schnapps that had been brought over by the German soldiers.

Today, I do drink socially. I can say that I stay away from hard liquor as much as possible; I've lost the taste for it and the "need" for it as well. Of course, there is always a night here and there that some of my friends do ask me to take a shot of tequila with them. This probably only happens a handful of times throughout the year, and I've gotten fairly good at saying no.

The Border Patrol

. . . .

A few months before leaving Fort Riley, Kansas, and completing ten years of military service, I applied for the United States Border Patrol (USBP). I didn't truly know much about the Border Patrol when I first applied. I had done some research on it and thought it would be in my best interest to continue on with some form of government service. Unfortunately, the USBP was in the middle of a two-year hiring freeze when I applied. It took exactly two years for them to finally call me and offer me a job.

During that time, I had moved to Temple, Texas, had remarried and had another son. My son was born on May 5, 2005, Cinco de Mayo. My newborn son was named after me and was born around 4:30 p.m.; it would have been awesome if he was actually born at 5:00 p.m. I had also begun working as a finance representative for Nextel Communications. I was promoted to supervisor within my first year of employment.

I remember, a few months before actually getting the call from the USBP, I had started to exercise and run again. Okay, maybe *run* is too strong of a word; I was jogging. What can I say? I still hated to run, yet I applied for a job where I would have to run after people. What a genius. There were times during my jog that I would remember my last few months in the army. During those months, I kept looking forward to never having to run again. I could not wait for my final day in the army; I had told myself that I would never run after my military service. I just hated it that much. Well, still do. Whenever I would remember those days, I would start laughing at myself while I was jogging down the street. I'm sure that the passersby would see me laughing and wonder what the hell was wrong with me. Who wouldn't wonder what the hell was wrong with the big Mexican guy who was laughing as he ran on the side of the road?

The USBP called me during the last days of October 2005. I was at work when I received the phone call. I was given two options for duty station: Laredo, Texas, or Falfurrias, Texas. I knew Falfurrias would be the closest I could get to my hometown, Weslaco, Texas, and I had already heard plenty of bad things about Laredo. The decision was easy; I selected Falfurrias. I submitted my resignation at work and reported back to the Rio Grande Valley in South Texas two weeks later.

I took my oath of service on November 14, 2005, and reported to the academy for training in Artesia, New Mexico, the following day. Training at the academy was tough. We had to learn immigration law, nationality law, proper Border Patrol Spanish (the proper terminology to use out in the field), physical training, firearms training, emergency driving, and arrest techniques. I will venture to say that the same shenanigans I had experienced during the army's Basic Training Course were experienced there. The difference was that it was done in a much more politically correct manner. Either way, some of the situations I went through at the academy were fairly funny, when I think about them now.

My class, the 606th Session, was comprised of fifty trainees from all over the country with the vast majority actually being from the state of Texas. Our instructors separated the class into two separate groups, and each group was assigned a section leader. The section leader is always a trainee from the same class that is normally selected by either the operations or law instructors and, at times, the physical training instructor. I was selected to be the section leader for my group. When you're trying to remain focused on your studies and all other training aspects at the academy, being the leader of your section is not an easy job.

All eyes are always on the trainees, especially the new class; so if anyone from your class messes up, the leader is the first to be reprimanded for it. Having been a sergeant in the army made my task easier with regard to keeping everyone informed and in step when marching. But this was not the military, and I couldn't just yell at an individual and expect full cooperation or obedience. For everything I ever addressed with the group or any individual, I received plenty of feedback. Emotions and attitudes ran high for a lot of individuals in my class, and it made for a very interesting four months.

Physical training was the one class where I always seemed to get into some form of shit. I recall one morning, during our run, I was lagging in the back of my section, and one of my instructors came up next to me.

"Mr. Tinoco, aren't you the section leader of this group?"

"Roger that, sir!"

"Who the hell is Roger, Mr. Tinoco? Did I ever introduce myself to you as Roger?"

"No, sir! Bad habit from the army, sir!"

"Holy cow, Mr. Tinoco! You mean to tell me that you were in the military and you can't even keep up with your group?"

Shit, I couldn't tell him that I hated to run. That would lead to some other crazy stuff.

"No, sir. I'm not saying that I can't keep up!"

"Oh, you're not, huh? So this must be your leadership style then! Is that it? This is the type of leader you are? You like leading from the rear?"

Being the smart-ass individual that I am, I couldn't help it.

"Well, yes, sir! This way, I can keep my eyes on the entire group and see how they're doing!" I actually wanted to laugh after I said this.

"Oh shit, Mr. Tinoco! Are you telling me that you are out here doing my job? You're saying I don't know what the hell I'm doing as a PT instructor! Oh, I got something for you, sir!"

As soon as he finished saying that, he took off in a full sprint to link up with the lead instructor of the class. A minute later, the whole group was in the sand, doing push-ups, sit-ups, and flutter kicks. The group knew I had been the one to get them in trouble. Our instructors were never shy about letting the entire group know who the cause of their pain was.

A week or so later, we were inside the mat room, where we would normally do calisthenics. On that particular day, we were learning about officer presence. This is our first form of force to try to effectuate an arrest. We must be able to portray confidence and assertiveness when giving an individual verbal commands.

Our lead instructor was asking us about a specific acronym that we needed to follow whenever we were dealing with an individual who might appear to be hostile or any person whom we've already determined is going to be arrested.

"Can anyone here tell me what the acronym ATM stands for?"

Nobody was raising their hand. Being of Mexican descent, I knew, as everyone else in the room did, that we always use a phrase whenever we want to state that something or someone is awesome or if a situation is "all good." In most cases, we use the phrase with its more vulgar connotation, which would mean "fucking awesome." So I raised my hand; I knew the answer to that question.

"Mr. Tinoco, what does the acronym ATM stand for?" I smiled confidently as I answered the question. "It means *a toda madre*, sir."

I could hear all my classmates around me trying hard not to laugh as they suppressed their giggles. Even the instructor wanted to laugh, but he couldn't since he had to remain professional and didn't want to lose control of the situation. After all, we were learning about officer presence.

"Wrong, sir! The acronym stands for ask, tell, make." Okay, so I was way off on that one.

"Ask, tell, make" is what we must follow whenever we are about to effect an arrest or subdue an individual. This is done in order to minimize our actual use of force in any given situation. We ask the individual to do what we want. When that doesn't work, we tell the individual to do what we want. And finally if the individual is still not being compliant, we make the individual do what we want (ask, tell, make).

My training continued on until the end of March 2006. The class I was in lost several trainees in the process due to medical issues and for failure to pass some of the exams. Throughout training, there were some instances when I would get upset over something stupid that my classmates had done or if a particular deficiency had already been addressed and they continued to make the same mistakes. On those occasions, I would tend to address the class as though I were still a sergeant addressing my soldiers. I knew I wasn't getting anywhere with them when I would get their dumbfounded looks that asked, "Who the fuck is this guy?" Whenever I saw that, I would revert to a more subtle approach and all would be okay.

Our training wasn't over when we graduated though. All of us were sent to our respective duty stations, and we still had to undergo additional training. We had to learn the area we were working and our different operations. Some of my classmates had been assigned to river stations that are located near the Rio Grande River. Out of the ten individuals who were assigned to the Falfurrias, Texas, Border Patrol Station, only five of us made it past the academy. At the end of our first year at the station, only three of us remained. We had been assigned to the busiest immigration checkpoint in the nation. This checkpoint is located approximately thirteen miles south of Falfurrias, Texas, on Highway

281 and about seventy miles north of the United States-Mexico border. Upon our arrival at the station, we quickly found out that we had to learn about brush, foot-sign tracking operations, highway operations, processing undocumented aliens, and checkpoint operations.

Something unexpected took place when I first moved back to the city of Weslaco, Texas. I went to go visit my dad (grandfather). I wanted to spend some time with him, and I was curious to know what he thought of my new job. My mother was supportive but also a bit concerned. She was still living in Reynosa, Mexico, at that time, and she wasn't too sure on how to address my new employment. Could she talk about it with her friends or was the topic completely off limits? What would her friends think of the fact that her only son's new job was to catch and deport Mexicans who were living in the United States illegally? I had not considered what my family would think about my choice in career. Living so close to the border and still having family living in Mexico made things a bit strange. In general, everyone was happy that I was finally going back home. I had been away from the Rio Grande Valley for twelve years. They just had some mixed emotions about the job I now had. They were proud but a bit hesitant to be "excited" about it.

The day I visited my dad, I showed up in my BP uniform; I wanted to surprise him and also see for myself what he thought of my new job. He still lived in the same small house where he and my grandmother had raised me. I found him watering his small garden as I pulled into the driveway. He stopped momentarily to see who had arrived and began to smile once he realized it was me. I opened the door to my truck, got out, and began to walk toward him. His smile slowly became something else. Something I had never seen on him. It wasn't sadness, it wasn't fear, and it surely wasn't amazement. I had truly never seen or expected that look on my dad's face, yet he slowly regained his color and his smile as I reached him, hugged him, and gave him a kiss on the cheek.

As our embrace broke, he asked me to sit down, and I helped him onto his rocking chair prior to sitting down myself.

"Está bien, 'Apa?" Are you okay, Dad?

"Sí, mijo, pero recorde muchas cosas cuando te vi en uniforme." Yes, son, but I remembered so many things when I saw you in uniform.

That was strange to me. I didn't recall my dad ever telling us any stories of dealing with the Border Patrol when he was young. We all knew he had initially entered the United States illegally but then did what was required to obtain his Resident Alien status to be able to live and work here without fear of ever being removed back to Mexico.

"Qué recuerdos, 'Apa?" What memories, Dad?"

He looked at me as if trying to determine whether or not he should tell me about the memories I had stirred up for him. It was a long, quiet moment, and I could tell he was struggling with his decision. My dad had always been a man of few words, but I had never seen him struggle with words.

He began to rock back and forth on his rocking chair as he began to tell me about his younger years as an undocumented alien. He told me he would enter the country illegally once every two weeks or so. He said that most of the BP agents he ever encountered or that ever arrested him were fairly nice. He talked about how none of the agents had ever given him reason to fear them, yet he always felt terrified whenever he was caught.

"Ellos sabian que solo venia a trabajar. Unos de ellos ya me conocian y me llamaban por mi nombre cada vez que me miraban." They knew I was only coming to work. Some of them already knew me and would call me by my name whenever they saw me.

He talked for a long time about how he would have to use different spots along the Rio Grande to swim across and enter the country. He did so in an attempt to find the unguarded areas and be able to come work.

"Cada día que me agarraban, era un día perdido. Y cada día perdido, era un día sin dinero para poder comer." Every day they caught me was a day lost. And every day lost was a day without money to eat.

As he continued to tell me his stories, tears began to roll down his face. He choked up a few times with his words yet wouldn't stop talking. It was as if he needed to get those things off his chest. As if he had held on to those memories all his life and finally found an outlet to relieve himself of them.

"Ellos nunca me trataron mal. Era como un juego de niños, un juego de escondite." They never treated me bad. It was like a child's game, a game of hide-and-seek.

"Pero siempre les tuve miedo. Eran mucho mas altos que yo, y cargaban unas pistolas grandisimas. Tambíen me daba mucho miedo por que los coyotes siempre nos decian que si La Migra nos pescaba, nos iban a golpear y talvez matar. Nos decian que La Migra nos odiaba a los Mexicanos." I always feared the Border Patrol. They were much taller than I was and would always carry their big guns. I was also afraid because the smugglers would always tell us that we would be beaten and possibly killed by the Border Patrol if they ever caught us. They would tell us that the Border Patrol hated Mexicans.

He stopped momentarily to wipe his tears away and regain his composure. I took the moment to get him a glass of water from inside the house. It seemed so much smaller than when I was living there. Walking into and then back out of the house was such a surreal moment. He looked up at me as I handed him the glass of water and smiled. In that instant, I remembered our short drive on the day he had bought me my first car. I saw that same sense of ease and amazement that I had seen all those years ago when I was just seventeen. I was so ready to break down in that instance. I held it together.

As I sat back down, he drank some water and then leaned toward me. He placed his glass of water on the ground and grabbed my hands.

"Estoy contento por ti, mijo. Estoy orgulloso de ti. Te digo estas cosas por que yo te vi crecer y se que tu vas a ser igual de bueno como aquellos oficiales que me pescaban a mi." I'm happy for you, son. I'm proud of you. I tell you these things because I saw you grow up and know that you will be just as kind as those officers that would catch me.

All the things I had ever encountered in my life up to that moment had never prepared me for the immense flow of emotions that ran through me in that instant. I broke down along with him as he continued to smile at me. Images of us picking crops in Michigan ran through my mind. Memories of cold mornings, picking oranges and grapefruit in the Rio Grande Valley, surfaced as well. My grandmother's argument, which kept me from joining the Marines, came to light once more. The many days and nights of missing my mother while I was here and she remained in Mexico, struggling to survive on her own. I looked at our house, such a tiny house; how could eight of us possibly live and be raised in that house?

I was shaking as I turned back toward my dad. His loving smile was still beaming brightly on his face. This frail yet strong man who had forced me to learn so much at such a young age. This man who had instilled his work ethic in me. He too had struggled for his kids to live a better life than his own. He too had broken the cycle from his own parents by taking so many chances in coming to the United States. He too had left his parents and siblings behind in search of something better. As poor and humble as we had been throughout all those years, he had found that better life. Seeing him in that instant, I finally realized this, and I believe that, seeing me in uniform at that moment, he too finally realized it. All my life, I had fought hard against my entire family to do more, to leave the house and my hometown to see if the world had a better life to offer. All that time, my grandparents had been doing the same thing. I was—no, I am my grandfather's youngest son, and I am exactly like him.

This revelation was excruciatingly overwhelming. My grandfather, my dad had been one of the strongest people I had ever known. He had fought me on so many things while I was growing up. He had placed so many obstacles in front of me, and I had always found a way to overcome them. All he was doing was to prepare me for the struggles that lay ahead of me. To say that I am forever grateful is an understatement. All those years, I thought I was looking at someone and seeing flaws that I wanted to overcome or improve. It turned out that I was seeing someone I wanted to emulate; I wanted to be exactly like him.

Unknown to me on that day, I would be tested by an old family acquaintance and longtime neighbor. In the months that followed, I continued to learn more about my own job. It was all on-the-job training, and I was actually enjoying everything I was doing at work. I would go visit my dad from time to time and share my own stories with him. He would always get a good laugh out of some of them and would, of course, caution me on some of the stories as well.

One thing about our job as agents is that we can be recognized at any given time. There are times when that recognition can be a good thing, and then there are times when it can be a bad thing. I think that, for many of us, this became prevalent after the National Geographic Channel aired the television series *Border Wars*. This series showcased many rescues, arrests, and cases that agents of the Customs and Border Protection Agency encounter on a daily basis. Working at a checkpoint with such high traffic only adds to the number of occurrences that an agent is recognized.

The checkpoint portion of the job can be fairly stressful at first. Pedestrians drive up to the checkpoint as they are driving farther into the country. During their temporary stop, we conduct our immigration inspection. The inspection itself takes less than a minute; in most cases, it takes approximately twenty to thirty seconds to complete. During that short time, we must conduct a visual search of the occupants, the vehicle, and all visible items within. While doing so, we also inquire as to the nature of their travel and their immigration status in country. Are they United States citizens, and if not, do they have the necessary immigration documents that allow them to be and or remain in country?

The stressful part of the job is being able to establish some form of suspicion that something is amiss. Are the immigration documents counterfeit or not? Are the bearers of those documents the true owners, or are they impostors? Is everyone in the vehicle answering the agent's questions honestly? Do the answers of the occupants and the complete picture they are portraying to the agent match up, or are they in sync? All these questions and more are addressed at what seems to be the speed of light and thus can be fairly stressful and frustrating when first learning the trade.

The agent conducting the inspection is working together with a Border Patrol canine handler. The canine handler is allowing his partner, the canine, sniff the exterior of the vehicle, in search of a particular scent the canine has been trained to detect. If one of those specific odors is detected, the canine will alert and grant us the probable cause necessary to physically search the vehicle and its occupants. If this happens, the vehicle is referred to a designated area for a secondary inspection. During that inspection, we must confirm or dispel the suspicion that was developed at primary when we initially made contact with the vehicle and its occupants.

A few years back, an old family acquaintance had either seen me in uniform or seen me at work one day and decided to let me know of his stupid intentions. The man had apparently gone to school with one of my brothers and knew my entire family. One evening while visiting my dad, this idiot decided to stop by the house as I was getting ready to leave. I got into my truck and noticed a vehicle stop behind me and blocked me from exiting my dad's driveway.

"Tinoco! Hey, Tinoco!"

I wondered who it was and didn't think much of it since the person was calling out my name and I was visiting the old colonia (neighborhood). So I got off my truck and made my way toward the vehicle that was blocking me. It turned out to be an old neighbor of ours from when I was a kid. I came up to his passenger window, which was already open, and said hello again.

"Hey, Tinoco. Visiting your dad?"

"Yeah, man. What's up?"

"Not much, man, I saw that you were here and decided to stop by to talk."

That was strange. Our families had never gotten along together. My grandparents didn't allow any of us to hang out with them when we were younger. Reason being that they were in the business of selling marijuana.

"Yeah? Talk about what?"

"Well, it's funny how things in life turn out, isn't it?"

"What do you mean?"

"I mean, here I am, doing what I do, keeping the family business going, and there you are working at the checkpoint that I have to drive through all the time."

I had started to get irritated. I could feel the anger building up in me as I listened to the idiot.

"I guess you can see it that way."

He laughed out loud. I didn't see what the hell was so funny.

"Well, Mr. Border Patrol lawman! Let me tell you something!"

He leaned closer toward the passenger window with a stupid huge grin on his face.

"I know your dad lives here by himself. I also know where all your brothers and your sister live. So from here on out, whenever I go through your checkpoint, I better be allowed to just drive on through! Do you understand, *pinche* Migra [fucking Border Patrol]?"

It took everything in me to control the rage that ran through my body in that moment. I kept telling myself to be cool, be calm. I had just started this career, and the last thing I needed was to be fired for beating the crap out of some lowlife asshole. I couldn't believe that this piece of shit had just threatened my entire family and right outside of my dad's house!

In a controlled yet strained voice, I addressed his threat.

"Look, man. I don't give a shit that you know where my entire family lives. I don't give a shit about you nor the rest of your piece-of-shit family. But if you ever come through my checkpoint, you better not be carrying anything you're not supposed to, because I am going to pull your fucking rig to the side and check every fucking inch of it. Do I make myself clear?"

He pulled back a bit. I don't think he had expected that response from me.

"So that's how it's going to be, *pinche* Migra?"

"That's exactly how it's going to be, motherfucker! If I catch you with something at the checkpoint, I will arrest your stupid ass!"

"Well, we'll see about that, Tinoco!"

He placed his truck in gear and drove off at high speed. I couldn't believe what had just taken place. I was shaking all over with anger. My adrenaline was running high, and it took me a few moments to regain my composure. My dad had heard the vehicle drive off and stepped out of the house.

"Quien era, mijo?" Who was it, son? I turned toward my old man.

"Era un idiota, 'Apa." It was an idiot, Dad.

I walked over toward him and explained what had just happened. I told him that I would call work and report the incident. I asked him not to worry and told him that everything would be taken care of. Somehow, he believed me.

As I was leaving his house, I immediately called one of my supervisors from work. I briefed him on what had just transpired and asked him what else I needed to do. He told me not to worry about it until I got back to work the next day. I was told to go ahead and write down everything in a memorandum the next day at work and turn it in to him. I then called one of my brothers and told him about it as well. I asked him if he knew the idiot's complete name. Luckily, he did. I jotted down the complete name and took it to work with me the following morning.

At the station, I once again briefed my supervisor of the incident and went over the memorandum with him once it was complete. He read it, pushed it up the chain of command, and they in turn reached out to other local law enforcement agencies for assistance.

Fifteen minutes later, my supervisor advised me that one of the other agencies had called back. They had read the memo and queried the idiot's name through their own database. They had an image available and wanted me to go in to see if I could identify the man who had made the threat. My supervisor and I both went down to their office and met with an officer there. Pleasantries were exchanged, and they quickly showed me a picture. It was, in fact, that same idiot. Apparently, he had already been arrested in the past for transporting narcotics. The officer told me that they would check into it and asked that I notify them immediately should I ever come across the man again.

A week passed, and while I was checking traffic at the checkpoint, the same man stopped at my lane for an inspection. The asshole saw me and started laughing and wanted to talk as though nothing had taken place between us. I kept the encounter professional, conducted my inspection, and then called for a supervisor over the radio. It just so happened that my field operations supervisor (FOS) had stopped by the checkpoint to see how things were going that day. He made his way out to my inspection lane. I stepped to the side momentarily and informed him that the guy in the eighteen-wheeler was the same person who had threatened my entire family the previous week. With that said, the eighteen-wheeler was directed toward the secondary inspection area, and everything was inspected again. The entire rig was checked out. Nothing was found.

As soon as my FOS and the other agents were done searching the vehicle, the guy was released and allowed to continue on his way. My supervisor called the local agency again and notified them of the incident. All of us thought the same thing; that asshole had probably decided to test me and see if I would just wave him on through without actually conducting an inspection. Well, I don't think he got the results he was after.

A few days later, the officer called the checkpoint, looking for me. The officer wanted my supervisor and me to make our way back down to their office. We immediately jumped into one of our units and drove down there. Upon our arrival, we were briefed by the officer who had taken over my case. He said that the guy was seen at his residence and that we were about to pay him a visit. He did tell us that at no time were we to exit our vehicle; unless it was a matter of officer safety, we were to remain inside our vehicle the entire time.

To my surprise, we joined in on a slew of vehicles from various different law enforcement agencies. It seemed as though the entire Rio Grande

Valley Law Enforcement Community were part of the caravan making its way to the idiot's residence. When we got there, my supervisor and I remained in our vehicle while everyone else got off. We had filled that street with government vehicles. It was strange to be back in my old colonia in a "working capacity." Within a few minutes, a lot of commotion began coming out of the residence. A whole lot of cursing and yelling, along with a few things being broken inside, could be heard.

Then, as if nothing had taken place, all the different officers came back out and got back into their respective vehicles. Nobody was being hauled out of the residence. The officer made his way to our vehicle and talked to us. He told us that the guy would never bother me or anyone else in my family again. The idiot had made himself a target, and everyone involved believed that he would be walking a very straight line from that day on. I can't say that the guy hasn't done anything illegal ever since that day, but I can say that he has never gotten near anyone in my family since then. The Border Patrol had backed me up and taken care of the threat with the help of every other law enforcement agency in the area.

There are many who think the agency will not take care of them. There are many who think corruption is understandable when an agent's life and family are threatened.

I believe them to be incorrect.

TINMAN

. . . .

In the military, I'm just as sure that, in every line of work in the country and possibly the world, nicknames are given to individuals for either their personality, something great they've accomplished, or even something stupid.

It is no different in the Border Patrol. I know agents who have earned nicknames such as Spooky, Jake the Snake, Spider-Man, Highpockets, Tiny, Tali, El Dude, Chief, and even M&M, just to name a few. Most of their stories are hilarious, while others are just simple depictions of the person who has earned that particular nickname. M&M, for example, is always utilized for those agents who just love to tell lies about all the great things that they've ever done or all the important people they know. We use the acronym M&M for Mil Mentiras, "thousand lies." Those agents are funny because, no matter what war story is ever being discussed, they always have one better, have done something better, have been through something far worse, or know someone who has. We just can't help but listen to their crap because we always want to see how far they'll go with their stories.

Most times, though, agents earn nicknames for doing or saying something stupid. Those are always the good names and probably the most memorable ones. I have a classmate from the Border Patrol Academy whom we nicknamed Puss in Boots. The reason for his name comes after one drunken Friday night at the academy. The doors to our dorms would always lock automatically as soon as the door closed, so we always had to carry our keys with us. This classmate of mine decided to step outside to the ice machine one morning in nothing other than his boxers and boots. Yep, he forgot to take his key with him. Poor guy didn't get any help for a while. As his classmates, we had to, of course, ignore his pleas whenever he came over to our dorms, knocking on our doors and windows to let him in. We left him out there in his boxers and boots for a while. The name has stuck ever since.

Jake the Snake is another name that was earned from one of those embarrassing moments. This agent is a good guy and a hard worker; unfortunately, he had a strange experience in the field and earned his name. To make matters worse, the poor guy's name isn't even Jake. When he was a trainee, he was out on the brush, tracking a group of undocumented aliens with his classmates and his field training officer. They were able to catch up to the group but had to give chase when everyone started running away from the agents. A lot of agents clip their radio mic onto the shoulder lapel of their uniform. When they start running, though, that mic does tend to come loose from the lapel and fall down. Luckily, the coiled wire that connects the mic to our handheld radios just causes for it to dangle loosely while running or walking. During this particular chase, the agent's mic did come loose and was dangling from his hip as he ran after the undocumented aliens. While giving chase, the agent felt something striking his leg repeatedly. This caused him to panic, thinking it was a snake that was trying to somehow attack him, and he began jumping up and down hysterically while yelling out, "Snake, snake, snake!" His FTO made his way toward him to see what was actually taking place and shortly after realized that the loose mic was the fearsome snake. Jake the Snake was born.

I have earned the nickname Tinman. I have been called Tinman for as long as I can remember. The true reason behind the name has been lost through the many variations of the story. One theme has remained constant, though. The Tinman has no heart.

Through time, even I have changed the reasoning behind my nickname. Yet there is some truth to my version of the story. It can be said that I was given this nickname simply because of the first three letters of my last name, Tinoco. Instead of calling me by my actual name, agents chose to call me Tinman. It does lend to the fact that so many people have a tough time pronouncing my last name.

It can also be said that I am just a mean person. Which in many cases, I am. I have been known to be an asshole when it comes to expecting individuals to do the right thing. So many of us work in this great agency. There should be no reason for any agent to be allowed to go through the system for not working. I simply have no respect for lazy individuals or individuals who are able to talk their way out of actual work on a daily basis. Especially when it would have taken far less time and effort to actually do the work. To those individuals, yes, I am an asshole. Suck asses; people who choose to kiss ass the entire way up the chain have a pretty tough time dealing with me as well.

If asking a person to pull their weight and do the job they have sworn to do makes me a heartless person, then yes, I am definitely heartless. If calling a person out for slacking on the job all the time and then lying to management about all the hard work they've done makes me a heartless person, then yes, I am heartless. If holding a new agent or trainee to a high standard and expecting them to perform their duties accordingly make me a heartless person, then yes, I am that heartless Tinman.

Some agents actually describe me as a quiet person. Some will actually laugh at this statement, my wife included. Some know that I am fairly quiet until it's time for the madness to shine through. Like everywhere else, there is a lot of trash-talking in the patrol. Some agents like to take small, quick jabs at others when they are talking trash. Those individuals normally learn about my trash-talking the hard way. I have been told that, when someone throws a jab at me, I come back swinging. Once again, these matters are all best left for those around me to address. I can only state the different things I am told and hear from time to time. In any case, it's all in good fun.

The story I like is that of being an asshole to the local criminals whom we encounter daily, especially those I used to deal with when working at the Falfurrias checkpoint. When an agent comes across a smuggling case, whether it be human trafficking or narcotics, it is up to that agent and his or her canine handler partner to interview all the individuals involved and develop a case strong enough for criminal prosecution. Some of the criminals encountered are easy to interview and are actually fairly forthcoming with all the facts of the criminal act they committed. Others are a bit tougher to break.

I would actually do my best to try to get the criminals to cry and then voluntarily give me all the facts concerning their crime. None of this would be done by using force. All of it would be done by way of conversation. Some of the conversations were heartless in nature, of course. It is through effective use of those heartless conversations and interviews that I would get them to cry and divulge everything that was needed to prosecute them.

Yet the basic fundamental truth behind my nickname stems from my very first arrest that had to do with fraudulent immigration documents.

As Border Patrol agents, we are required to learn everything possible about all the immigration documents that are utilized today. We must know about their security features, their specific fonts, color schemes, layouts, information formats and have an in-depth understanding of which individuals should be carrying a specific type of document to be or remain in the United States.

Coming across a document and quickly scanning it to determine its legitimacy and then comparing the image of the person on the document to the actual individual who is presenting it can be a pretty daunting task. It's important to remember that agents working at the checkpoint don't have all day to check a document. Everything happens at the speed of light. This is more evident when checking commercial buses that have twenty or more passengers on board.

I was still considered a trainee when this particular arrest took place. I had boarded a commercial bus to conduct an immigration inspection of all its passengers. While I asked the passengers for their immigration documents I realized how overwhelming the situation actually was. I was fairly new at the job and wanted to prove myself to the senior agents working in my unit. I kept grabbing and visually scanning documents as I went through the bus, questioning individuals and trying to observe everything and everyone on board. Then, I came across a document that I knew was fake. The adrenaline began flowing through me as I got excited for having caught my first fake document.

In my excited state, I failed to catch and control a basic human reaction. I got tunnel vision, and I failed to control it.

I kept looking at the document, knowing it was a fake. I looked at the individual who had presented it to me, yet I didn't really see the individual. Tunnel vision. I had gone in for the kill while the adrenaline was still running high through my body. The person who presented the fake document to me was a female. I informed the other agent on the bus with me that I was taking her in for the fake document. The agent just looked at me as though I were crazy. I still didn't catch his reaction to my statement and what was happening. I had zoned in on the fake document, and nothing else mattered to me.

My partner continued to inspect the remainder of the bus while I asked the female to grab her personal things and follow me off the bus. Once we were off the bus, I escorted the female across the lanes of traffic toward the checkpoint. Every agent who was working outside kept on looking at me as I escorted the female. It's safe to say that even the public that was driving by as they were released from primary inspection was looking at me and wondering, what the hell? As we neared the entrance to the checkpoint, several agents were outside by the door, and they too were giving me that look of "What the fuck?"

As I walked her into the checkpoint, all the agents began calling me out.

"Dang, Tinoco! You have no heart, bro."

"That's just plain cold, Tinoco!"

"What the hell, man? You're an asshole, bro!"

The female I had taken off the bus for having a fake immigration document was in fact an old lady that was over sixty years old.

Yes, I had arrested a grandma.

In my defense, she might have been the Wicked Witch of the East! No heart.

Tinman.

Falfurrias

·················

The Falfurrias Border Patrol Station is a very unique place. The work there is unlike anything else I've ever encountered. Agents are able to patrol through various large ranches with some of the most well-known being the King Ranch, Cage's Ranch, La India, Mariposa, the Jones Ranch, and the Vickers' Ranch, to name a few. Working in these ranches and others can be dangerous at times. Many undocumented aliens (UDAs) have perished inside some of those ranches in their attempt to circumvent the Falfurrias Border Patrol Checkpoint. They take their chances of walking through the high brush, hoping to evade arrest and, ultimately, removal to their native country.

People from all over the world take their chances through those ranches, not knowing that the human traffickers they've paid don't care about them. Those pieces of shit only care about the money they are making. They lie to the people about their chances of survival. Some of them rape women of all ages as they're being guided through the brush to what they hope will end up being a better life for them. These smugglers hold people hostage in an attempt to get more money out of their families.

For the most part, some of the brush guides who are used are always high on some form of narcotic so that the fast hike through the brush won't bother them as much. Yet the UDAs who are following behind must endure the hike with a minimum amount of water and food. I have come across groups of UDAs who had run out of water and had reverted to drinking filthy water used by the cattle on the ranches. If an individual gets hurt during the hike or can't keep up with the rest of the group, they are left behind to fend for themselves. Some of them are able to make it out to the main highway and get picked up by us, while others are not so lucky.

Some of those individuals who are not able to make it out of the ranches end up losing their lives due to dehydration, exhaustion, hunger, and at times, due to an injury they had sustained through the hike. Yes, the smugglers, who are more commonly referred to as coyotes, never give a damn about a person who sustains an injury. They too are left behind to fend for themselves. There are a number of individuals who are fortunate enough to keep their mobile phones on them. Should they ever be left behind or be not able to keep up with the brush guide, they are able to make a 911 call for help.

Whenever any of our Border Patrol stations receive a 911 call from a UDA who is lost in the brush, we do our best to locate those individuals. All available assets are utilized to search for and, hopefully, rescue those people.

One of the best skills an agent can develop for the brush is that of sign-cutting and tracking individuals. Some of the areas that I've worked in are fairly desolate areas and fairly difficult to get to with a vehicle. All-terrain vehicles are utilized as well, but we deal with so many different ranches, and the fences that divide them only end up being a constant obstacle that slows us down. Tracking for individuals is something that I thoroughly enjoyed while working at the Falfurrias station.

Finding an individual's foot sign is only the beginning of the challenge. As an agent, we must be able to quickly determine whether the footprints we are looking at are fresh or if that group is already long gone. If we determine them to be fresh, we begin to track them. Tracking a group of individuals gives agents an insight into everything these people go through to try to elude us. We go through the same terrain they go through. It could be sandy, it can be a patch of swamp land, a fairly dry riverbed, and it can also be some extremely dense brush. Nighttime operations become even more challenging. We must practice light and noise discipline as much as possible. We do light up from time to time and make sure that we are still on the group's trail. Unfortunately, a bright light can be seen from great distances in the middle of the night. The use of all-terrain vehicles makes the noise discipline obsolete. A group of undocumented aliens can hear us coming a mile away. This means that we have to be quicker in determining the age of footprints and then track them as fast as possible since our headlights and noise give us away and we lose the element of surprise.

Constant communication with our partners and any other assets working with us is very important. Sometimes it is the one thing that can save our asses if we ever run into a situation that requires additional manpower. As a Border Patrol agent, tracking and catching up to a group can mean that we may end up effecting the arrest of ten or more individuals by ourselves. This is where our officer presence truly matters. We never know whom we are arresting. We catch individuals with extensive criminal records on a daily basis. We also deal with sex offenders, dangerous gang members such as MS-13, and people with active warrants for various crimes. Not everyone we track, catch up to, and apprehend has the good intentions of simply wanting to work.

Even the individuals without criminal histories can become dangerous encounters. It is important to understand that the people we deal with on a daily basis have left everything behind them in their native countries. Most have sold everything they ever owned in order to pay their way into the United States. In the end, a Border Patrol agent is the final obstacle who is keeping them from reaching their destination and dreams of a better life. This can and, most times, does become a last moment of desperation for them. Their arrest means they've sacrificed everything only to be removed back to their country of origin. Many are willing to fight through that, fight through us.

The largest group I ever caught was of fifty-four individuals. I didn't catch the group by myself. I had other agents working with me, and all of us were able to round them up. I had been working with two other senior agents, Ruben and Wiley, and the checkpoint had received a call that several minivans had dropped off a large group of individuals on

Highway 77. We didn't have an exact location of the drop-off, so the three of us had to cut for sign (look for footprints) along the road. All three of us were driving solo in our respective vehicles.

After a few minutes of sign-cutting, I was able to find some footprints and called Ruben over to verify and confirm that they were fresh. I was fairly new at that time and felt more comfortable asking Ruben for assistance with reading the footprints. He had been in service for over fifteen years already. Ruben drove over to my location to take a look and told me that it didn't look hot at all. Hot equals fresh. Ruben was great with one-liners. Whenever he would find fresh sign, he would call it out over the radio as "hot as fresh baked biscuits in the morning."

Since Ruben had stated the sign wasn't fresh, we continued to look around for other footprints. After a few minutes of not finding anything else in the vicinity, I decided to go back to the sign I had shown Ruben. Once I got to it, I decided to begin tracking it. I figured I had nothing to lose anyway. I remember telling Ruben over the radio that I was going to follow the sign for a bit to see if it led to anything. I got off my vehicle, made sure I had all my gear, jumped over the fence and into the ranch, and began tracking the footprints. The more I walked, the hotter the sign got. I called Ruben over the radio again and told him the sign was getting better as I tracked it. He told me to keep on following it and he would try to go ahead of me in his vehicle to see if he could come up with the same footprints.

After about twenty minutes of tracking, I saw that the footprints went into a motte of trees. The trees created a thick cover overhead, and we normally find groups hiding and even resting underneath a good set of trees. The checkpoint called over the radio that air support had been requested to help us search for the group and they were on their way.

I continued to track the sign toward the motte of trees and called out my location to Ruben and Wiley. It took me about fifteen more minutes to make my way to the trees; I could already hear the helicopter getting near. The brush surrounding the trees was pretty thick. I ducked to go in and immediately saw four bodies lying down inside the motte. I got tunnel vision and rushed in.

When I got to the bodies, I realized they were asleep. I quickly sat on top of two of the bodies as I grabbed the other two by their collars. They were startled and shocked. I let go of one so that I could call out my location over the radio. Then, as I grabbed my radio mic, I noticed bodies. Bodies all around me. I was surrounded underneath this motte. I quickly got on the radio and called for the helicopter whom we used to refer to as Fox.

"Fox 23A, this is Fox 2212. I got the group underneath the motte! I say again, the entire group is underneath the motte!"

The helicopter pilot replied immediately.

"Hey, 2212. We need you to come out of the motte so that we can get visual. The trees in this area are pretty thick. We have no visual at this time."

Shit, shit, shit!

Okay, I had to think fast. I couldn't let the group see me panic. How could I not panic or get excited? This was my first big group, and I was by myself at the moment. All I could see were bodies, bodies all over the place. My adrenaline was on overdrive. I looked at the spot that I had crawled through and determined that I needed to go out the same way so that the chopper could see me. Problem was I didn't want to let go of the bodies I had already. I didn't want the group to scatter all over the place either. I did my best to regain my composure, control the adrenaline, and began addressing the group.

"Nadie se mueva, Patrulla Fronteriza!" Nobody move, US Border Patrol!

"No intentan correr! Estan rodeados! Y tenemos un helicoptero!" Don't try to run! You're surrounded, and we have a helicopter!

They didn't know it was just me at the moment. I bluffed, and it worked.

"Fox 23A, this is Fox 2212. I'm making my way out of the motte with two bodies."

I grabbed two of the guys by their clothes and dragged them out of the motte with me. The whole time I kept telling the rest of the group not to move. As I made my way out of the motte with the two bodies, I began searching for the chopper. I couldn't see it! Shit! I kept pulling on the two bodies until we made our way to a small break between the trees. I ordered the two guys I had to lie facedown and stay that way while I attempted to find the chopper and wave it down.

"Fox 23A, I'm out in a clearing. I can hear you nearby."

They kept flying for another minute or so until they saw me. I kept on pointing into the motte of trees as I told them over the radio that there was a large group underneath it. They confirmed they had visual of me and began guiding Ruben and Wiley toward my location.

When it was all said and done, we had a total of fifty-four UDAs with us.

There are many instances when any of my coworkers, male and female, find themselves in similar situations. In most cases, we do our best to have a partner nearby to help out and back us up. We do have a dangerous, thankless job. Only we know exactly how things can be while tracking an individual or a group of people. The uncertainty of not knowing what type of person we will encounter is something we deal with every single day. Are they individuals only searching for a better life and only wish to come into the United States to work? Are they criminals from their respective native country, trying to evade their own government or police force? Are they undocumented criminal aliens with extensive criminal histories who have been removed from the United States in the past? Lastly, are they terrorists or individuals with the intent of committing terroristic acts in the United States?

The basic answer is that, when we first encounter them in the field, on the highway, at a bus terminal, airport, or at the checkpoint, we don't know what they are.

As Border Patrol agents, we don't know if they do, in fact, believe to have already lost everything in their native countries and thus try to hurt us in an attempt to evade arrest. We don't learn anything about them until we actually begin to process them for removal. Yet all these groups of individuals have the ability and the potential to fight back at any given moment.

Rescues do take place on a daily basis though. I've been a part of rescues that have taken place in the desolate or dense areas of the ranches, on the highway, and at the checkpoint. As I'm sure the same can be said about all of law enforcement, there's never a dull moment, and no day is the same.

A rescue that comes to mind is that of one that took place on Highway 281. One can always see Border Patrol vehicles on that highway on any given day or night. The reason is that road is a main funnel of illicit traffic trying to make its way farther north and farther into the United States. In the last ten years or so, there has been far more involvement from other agencies such as State Troopers working for the Texas Department of Public Safety and local law enforcement from Brooks County. It is through our combined efforts that we've been able to rescue so many UDAs and hinder the illicit operations that are constantly targeting us on the road and in the brush. One night, I was working highway operations along with other agents. The station had received information from a concerned citizen that a dark-blue sports utility vehicle (SUV) with thick tires and chrome wheels was making its way north on Highway 281 in an attempt to drop off a load of UDAs somewhere south of the Border Patrol checkpoint. This is done daily so that the coyotes can then guide their cargo of UDAs through the brush in an attempt to circumvent the checkpoint and get picked up north of its location.

We had a unit positioned approximately fifteen miles south of the checkpoint. The agents in that unit were on the lookout for the SUV. Once the SUV was spotted, they were to follow it north and call it out to the rest of us working the highway. The plan was for all of us to eventually make contact with the SUV and safely escort it off the highway to conduct an immigration inspection and determine whether or not it was, in fact, the load vehicle.

At about ten o'clock that evening, our southernmost unit called out the SUV that matched the description given to us. The agents began to follow behind it as two other units and I began to position ourselves north of them in an attempt to intercept it and then safely conduct a traffic stop.

It turned out that two other agents in another vehicle were able to link up with the SUV and the trailing unit. So one unit was directly behind the SUV, and the other was driving alongside its driver's side. One of the agents called out over the radio that he could see a lot of bodies inside the vehicle. We were sure it was the load vehicle.

The SUV began to slow down drastically as it continued to make its way north along the road. The agents with it continued to call out their speeds and to inform us that the vehicle was driving extremely slow but not stopping. The agents had already initiated all their vehicles' emergency equipment: the siren and overhead red and blue lights. And still the SUV wouldn't stop. I was positioned up the road from them. I was off the main road, on the shoulder, just waiting for them. I could see all the red-and-blues coming my way as the agents continued to follow the SUV. As the caravan of vehicles drew closer to my location, I heard an agent yell out over the radio.

"Unit in front of us, move out of the way! There is no driver in the SUV! I say again, there is no driver in the SUV!"

It took me a second to react; what the hell did he mean there was no driver in the SUV? Once the reality of the message sank in, I immediately placed my vehicle in gear and moved out of the way. The caravan of vehicles was probably about fifteen feet from me when I hauled ass out of the way. As I drove out of my position, I was able to see an agent climbing out of the passenger window of the Border Patrol vehicle and was trying to jump into the SUV. What the hell was going on?

Moments later, the SUV stopped, and we had agents flying out of our units as we rushed over to the SUV in an attempt to contain everyone inside and make sure they were all safe. An agent was now in the driver's seat of the SUV. Once we made sure nobody had rushed out of the vehicle, we began to get everyone out one by one and had them sit down away from the road. We always do this in order to get a good count of the individuals we apprehend and begin our visual inspection of everybody to ensure nobody is hurt or injured in any way.

I could hear one of the agents asking everyone what had happened to the driver of the vehicle. Nobody was saying anything. I walked over to the vehicle and began inspecting it, along with other agents. One of them found a single shoe had been left behind underneath the gas pedal of the vehicle. We quickly went over toward the group and began looking for the person missing a shoe.

We found our driver. We now had a case and were able to prosecute the driver not only for the smuggling of UDAs, but also for the deadly risk he had placed all their lives in. That SUV could have easily veered toward another vehicle on the road or crashed against a tree with all those people inside. There was a total of fourteen people inside the SUV that night.

Never a dull moment.

Rescues at the checkpoint are even more commonplace. There probably isn't a day that goes by without agents finding people hiding inside the trunks of vehicles in extremely hot weather. There was a time when we ended up rescuing a man from burning near the engine of a pickup truck. The smugglers had changed out the engine of a large truck and placed a smaller engine on it. This was done to make enough room to fit one person between the front grill of the truck and the radiator. None of us could believe it when we saw the man hiding there. I've seen people hiding inside speaker boxes, underneath floorboards, inside horse trailers, hiding within after-market compartments of cargo trailers, and even inside the frame of a flatbed trailer. Agents who work along the Rio Grande River see some of the same ruthless tactics used by smugglers. Some of the people who go across that river are not strong swimmers at all. Sometimes the coyotes take advantage of that situation, knowing that an agent will do what he or she can in order to save a person from drowning. Once the agent is occupied trying to save the person, the coyote is able to slip away and avoid being arrested.

I recall a man throwing a kid onto a cactus patch once. He did so with the sole intention of keeping us occupied in trying to rescue the kid while he ran away. The people I've encountered in the field have shown little to no regard for the safety of others when they are trying to get away from us. You would think that after ten years of working in the Border Patrol I would have already gotten used to seeing things like these. It may be hard to believe, but people always find a way to shock us with things we've never seen done before. I'll venture to say that we expect something crazy every day, but we just never know how crazy that something will actually be until we see it.

Although we do go through some serious situations on a daily basis, we also have plenty of lighthearted moments in the patrol. I recall a situation that involved two good friends of mine, Santiago and George. One night while working the midnight shift at the checkpoint, my two fearless buddies were partnered up to work highway operations. There are some moments during the midnight shift that can be fairly peaceful and quiet; this was one of those. At the checkpoint, we all monitor the service radio 24-7 so that we can listen for any requests from the agents out on the field or highway and be able to relay any important information while working traffic.

Our service vehicles are all equipped with a service radio as well, and the mic to that radio is normally positioned next to the driver's right leg. This does create a problem sometimes. The button utilized on the mic to speak may at times end up leaning against the driver's leg. When this happens, the driver unknowingly ends up pressing on that Talk button, and the entire station, the checkpoint, and our radio room end up listening to whatever is being said within that service vehicle.

This particular night was extremely quiet for some reason. Those of us working at the checkpoint were busy processing individuals, but everything was quiet nonetheless, and the radio we monitor seemed to be a bit louder than usual. All was peaceful until we heard Santiago come out over the radio, talking to George.

"Man, it's so big. Look at this thing."

The checkpoint was already quiet to begin with, but the moment we heard that statement come out over the radio, you could hear a pin drop.

Then George responded, "Dude, just put it in your mouth."

Normally, when agents have a "hot mic" situation, when they are unknowingly pressing on the Talk button, we quickly interrupt on the service radio and let them know that they have a "hot mic" so that they can adjust the radio mic and not be heard anymore.

None of us at the checkpoint or the station were doing that on this particular night. The conversation between Santiago and George was just too good to interrupt.

Santiago spoke again, "Bro, this is just way too much meat! I don't think it even fits in my mouth."

"Dude, don't tell me you're going to let all that go to waste. Just try it."

"George, I'll probably choke with it, man. I can barely wrap my hand around it."

"Quit playing around and just do it. It's not as big as it looks."

By this time, we were all trying so hard not to laugh out loud at the checkpoint and the station. Yet nobody was interrupting the conversation.

"I'm gonna have to go slow with this thing, man. It's too much."

"Dude, just put it in your mouth and enjoy the damn thing."

The radio went silent for a few seconds as we all waited to see what was going to be said next. George's voice came out. "Are you seriously going to let all that meat go to waste?"

"Yes, it won't fit. You saw that already."

Then we heard a cell phone ringing and George answering. A minute later, radio silence. Apparently, the radio room was also listening to their conversation and decided to give them a call to let them know of their "hot mic" situation.

Somebody always has to ruin a good thing. Later on, both Santiago and George came over to the checkpoint to explain the situation to us all. They were given all kinds of shit for it, of course. Their explanation was that Santiago had a huge sandwich with way too much meat in it and he ultimately made the decision to take some of the meat out of it so that he could eat it.

They did seem honest during their explanation, and it is possible. I mean, I'm sure we've all had moments when our spouse packs too much food for our lunch.

More Loss, Canines, and Training

· · · · · · · · · · · · · · · · · ·

After three years of working in the Border Patrol, I once again experienced loss. I received a phone call one morning from one of my brothers. My dad had passed away. I didn't know how to take the news at first. I couldn't believe it, for one, yet I felt guilty as hell. I couldn't even remember what our last conversation had been about. I still can't. For many reasons yet for no reason at all, my visits with him had become less frequent.

I say no reason at all because the realization of having lost him forever makes any possible reason seem petty and foolish. This was, after all, the man who had raised me. The one who passed on his work ethic to me. The one I had just realized a few years back had been my role model. The conversations I had enjoyed with him would be no more. Now only the memories remain.

I could blame it on the shift work and not having the time to actually go visit him. I could say that what little time I did have had to be spent with my own family and with my younger son. Although shift work is tough on agents and their families, I knew then as I know now, it was not the reason for my sporadic visits. I have no valid reasons; all I can say is that it happened and I must live with that.

The news of his passing actually came during a time that I was actually having a tough time at work and in my own house. At work, I was having a tough time and was looking for something else to do. I had already been involved in several highway and brush operations but was needing a different outlet to remain engaged and occupied. At home, things just weren't the same. Unknown to me at that time, I ended up getting separated and ultimately divorced just a few months after my father's passing. I once again felt I had lost everything. It was a dark time, for sure, but now I was wiser in the sense that I didn't feel the need to revert to drinking. I knew I had worked too hard for the career I now had. I just needed to figure things out again so that I could continue moving forward.

The Falfurrias station was in the process of increasing its number of canine handlers. Before applying for the opportunity, I had to consider the fact that I hadn't owned a dog since I was six years old. I didn't know anything about caring for a dog, much less working with one. I knew the Canine Training Center in El Paso, Texas, would train me and guide me on how to actually be partnered with a canine. I just wasn't sure if I could actually work with one.

The main reason for my concerns had to do with my dad. Now that I'm a parent, I can attest to the fact that there are times when parents can go overboard in showing their kids how much they care for them. I may be wrong, but I think some of us parents also tend to get tunnel vision when trying to make our kids happy that we lose sight of what we are actually doing. The whole dog incident with my dad is a perfect example of this. I know he didn't mean to scare the crap out of me at that time. I also know he truly believed there was nothing wrong with his actions; in his mind, he was doing what needed to be done in order to make me happy. Unfortunately, things didn't quite turn out how he wanted them to, and I ended up never wanting to own a dog again.

When I was six years old, I was barely in the first grade of elementary school. My parents had somehow acquired a dog for me to have as a pet. It was a German shepherd. There was one major catch to me having a pet, though, and my dad was dead serious about it.

"Este es tu perro," he told me. This is your dog.

"Nadie mas lo va cuidar. Si algo le pasa, es porque tu no lo cuidaste." Nobody else is going to take care of him. If something happens to him, it's because you didn't take care of him.

I was six years old and happy as hell that I had gotten a dog. Did he honestly believe that I was listening to his speech on being responsible for the dog? Did he honestly believe that I even knew what owning a dog entailed?

In short, yes, he did.

Our little house was not entirely fenced in. Why would it be? We didn't have money for such things. So part of my new responsibilities for owning a dog was ensuring every morning that the dog was secure in a way that it wouldn't run away or wander onto the street while I was at school. I remember having to walk outside to our back yard every morning before catching the school bus to ensure the dog was secured, had plenty of water and food.

One morning, I was running late. I had to walk down to the end of our street in order to catch the school bus. I knew it would be hell to pay if I missed the bus. That meant my dad would have to take me to school. That meant he would show up to work later, and less time in the fields always meant less money being earned. I left for school without ever checking on the dog.

That afternoon when I got home from school, my dad was outside waiting for me. I went up to him, kissed him on the cheek, and then went inside to change out of my school clothes. When I went back outside, my dad told me to sit down.

"Qué te dije sobre el perro?" What did I tell you about the dog?

"Que yo lo tenia que cuidar." That I had to take care of him.

"Y lo checaste en la mañana?" And did you check on him in the morning?

"No, 'Apa. Tenia miedo perder el bos." No, Dad. I was afraid to lose the bus.

"Pos el perro andaba suelto y salio a la calle. Lo machuco un carro." Well, the dog was loose and wandered out onto the street. A car ran over him.

I couldn't believe it. I looked over toward the street. It was empty, of course; my dad had already removed the dead dog. My dog, dead. I remember crying and feeling sad. My dad grabbed me and held me tight as he tried to console me. In my sobbing, I was able to hear the screen door of the house open. My grandmother had stepped out, and she made her way toward me as well. Both of them did their best to calm me down and, in their attempt, told me that they would get me another dog.

"Sí, mijo, yo te traigo otro perro. Solo dinos qué tipo de perro quieres e yo voy por el." Yes, son, I'll bring another dog for you. Just tell us what kind of dog you want, and I'll go get it.

I broke away from their embrace and made an attempt to stop sobbing as I wiped my tears away.

"Yo quiero un doberman." I want a doberman. They both looked at me, puzzled.

"Qué tipo de perro es ese?" What kind of dog is that?

"Es un perro flaco y negro con orejas picudas y la cola cortita." It's a skinny black dog with pointy ears and short tail.

"Está bien, quédate aquí en la casa mientras yo voy a buscarte ese perro." Okay, stay here at home while I go find that dog for you.

I cheered up a bit. All would be okay. I would be getting another dog; another pet for me to play with. I went back inside the house with my grandmother as my dad got into his pickup truck and drove away in search of a doberman for me. I didn't know where he was going. I figured he would be going to some store that sold dogs. When he showed up about two hours later, I was too excited that I didn't even care to ask him where he had gone to get the dog I had asked for.

I waited on our small porch anxiously as my dad got off his truck, opened up the camper, and pulled the dog out. It was a small black dog. I kept looking at it as my dad carried the dog toward me. He had a huge smile on his face; he must have been delighted as heck that he was about to make me a very happy kid. I think the bewildered look on my face caught him a bit off guard.

"Qué pasa? No te gusta el perro?" What's wrong? You don't like the dog?

"Sí, 'Apa, pero eso no es un doberman." Yes, Dad, but that's not a doberman.

"Como que no! Es negro como tu dijiste." What do you mean it's not? It's black just like you said.

"Sí, pero no tiene las orejas picudas y la cola cortita." Yes, but it doesn't have pointy ears and a short tail.

He looked at the dog in his arms and then looked at me with a huge grin on his face.

"No se preocupe, mijo. Eso ahorita lo arreglamos." Don't worry, son. We'll fix that shortly.

He handed the dog over to me and went back to his truck and pulled out some tools. I was busy playing around with the dog and didn't realize exactly what my dad had grabbed from the truck. A few minutes later, he came back to me and grabbed the dog. I saw a pair of scissors in his hand. "Ahora, Sergio. Necesito que cuides al perro fuerte mientras yo trabajo. Que no se mueva." Now, Sergio; I need you to hold the dog tight while I work. Don't let it move.

What? What for? I didn't really know what was going on, and I never bothered to even ask him. Before I knew it, my dad was cutting the dog's ears in order to make them pointy. Just as I had wanted them to be. Just like on a doberman.

The dog began wailing and thrashing in my small hands. I began crying and yelling the moment I saw the scissors clamp down on the dog's ear and blood began coming out. I was terrified. Why was he doing this to the dog? Why was he doing this to my dog?

"Que lo cuides te digo! No dejes que se mueva tanto!" Hold him I tell you! Don't let him move so much!

My dad was quick with the scissors and performed his mad-scientist act in a matter of seconds. I wanted to let go so badly. I didn't want to hold the poor dog anymore. I didn't want the dog at all, not like that!

My grandmother must have heard me crying again because she quickly walked out of the house to see what was going on. By the time she asked what was wrong, my dad had already cut off the dog's tail and had finished his horrible masterpiece.

"Juan, qué esta pasando? Porque esta llorando, Sergio?" Juan, what's happening? Why is Sergio crying?

"Pos yo que se? El queria un perro con orejas picudas y cola corta. Yo le corte las orejas y la cola al perro para que estuviera come el lo quiere. Fue lo que pidio." Well, what do I know? He wanted a dog with pointy ears and a short tail. I cut the dog's ears and tail so they could be like he wanted. It's what he asked for!

I ran toward my grandmother and held her tight, screaming, "Yo no quiero ese perro! Yo ya no quiero tener perro! No quiero nada!" I don't want that dog. I don't want a dog anymore! I don't want anything!

My grandmother scolded my dad for having butchered the poor dog.

Then she scolded him for having me help him. I was six years old, for crying out loud. She made my dad grab the dog and get rid of him. I don't know where he took him. I just know he left the house with a dog and came back without one.

It took thirty years for me to ever have another dog. Even then, the dog was for work. It took another six years to actually get a dog for a pet. I remember sharing this story with a buddy of mine, Adrian. We were postacademy instructors together for almost three years. We would laugh about it and wonder whether or not my dad had actually just stolen that poor dog from another neighborhood and then dropped him back off again all torn up. Anyone who might have seen the poor dog afterward had to have wondered what the hell had happened to him.

With that said, I became a canine handler in the Border Patrol. The thing about being a canine handler at the Falfurrias station was that, back then, the handlers were rarely allowed to work their canines out in the brush. I loved working in the brush, and thus, this became a huge drawback for me. Although I enjoyed being a canine handler, I didn't like being stuck working at the checkpoint every single day.

My canine's name was Bieko, and he was an awesome Belgian Malinois. When we first got back to the checkpoint after my training and certification, Bieko, like most dogs, was a bit scared of working next to all the vehicle traffic. The sounds of eighteen-wheeler air brakes going off next to us all the time, the heat of the exhaust, and the small work space that is available between lanes all play a role in the canine's effectiveness. As time goes by, most of the canines do get used to the conditions and are able to work without any issues. The first narcotics case that Bieko and I got was a small one. Fifty-three pounds of marijuana had been hidden inside the gas tank of an old Crown Victoria. Sadly, I wasn't able to properly praise Bieko for a job well done on alerting to the vehicle because we were sent out to back up a state trooper who was requesting canine assistance out on Highway 281. It was a good case, though, and I was able to locate the bundles, thanks to the help of another canine handler, Eleno. Fortunately, there is always a senior agent around to help whenever we start something new in the patrol. That's one of the great things about this agency.

In another occasion, an eighteen-wheeler had stopped for its immigration inspection. Bieko and I were working that particular lane along with the primary agent. I felt Bieko pull on his leash, and I followed him. He ran fast straight down to the rear of the eighteen-wheeler. I started thinking that the trailer was loaded with either bodies or narcotics. He hadn't pulled on me like that before. As soon as he got to the end of the trailer, he turned as though he were going to sniff on the seams of the back doors. I was wrong. Bieko kept on running past the doors and away from the checkpoint. There is a small fence on that side of the checkpoint. That small fence encloses a good portion of the King Ranch. Bieko ran toward it and jumped over it without missing a step. I was still holding on to his leash.

There was no way for me to jump over the fence, and I didn't want to pull on the leash either. I needed him to stay on whatever scent he had detected. I toppled over the damn fence and busted my ass in doing so. As I hit hard on the sand and ate some dirt, I lost my grip on the leash, and Bieko was gone. I got back on my feet and started running toward him as fast as I could. The only thought I had at that moment was losing Bieko. That would not have been a good thing, especially since I had only been a handler for such a short time. I yelled back toward the checkpoint, "Loose dog!" I could see where the high grass was breaking as Bieko ran through it. I kept on running behind him. I only ran for about fifty yards when I finally saw why he had run. Bieko was walking around a small group of UDAs. He kept looking up at them as though asking them where his toy was; he had, after all, done a good job in finding them. This was our first group; I'd say together, but it was all Bieko.

Our biggest case together was that of 8,400 pounds of marijuana being transported inside an oil tanker. I was working the midnight shift, and traffic was minimal. When that eighteen-wheeler showed up, Bieko just about lost his shit. He wanted to jump on that oil tanker. I didn't even bother with hand signals; it was just too obvious that Bieko had caught on to a very strong scent of something. I just told the primary agent, Nathan to go ahead and secondary the vehicle for further inspection. There weren't any other vehicles in the lane waiting for inspection at the time so Nathan and I both escorted the vehicle over to the secondary area.

Nathan quickly interviewed the driver with regard to his citizenship and what his destination was. The driver was headed to Houston, Texas. I ran Bieko again around the entire tractor and trailer, and he kept on wanting to climb onto the tanker. I told Nathan that I would stay with the driver and asked him to open one of the manholes on top of it for a visual inspection of the inside. As he took care of that, I remained with the driver and continued to probe him for information. I immediately knew he was full of shit.

"Where did you say you were taking this to?"

"Houston, Texas, sir."

"What are you hauling inside the tanker?"

"It's supposed to be water, sir."

Water inside an oil tanker with hazmat markings all over it. Really, guy?

"I didn't fucking ask you what you're supposed to have. I asked you what the fuck is in the tanker."

The Tinman had come out swinging. I've never cared for bullshit responses to simple questions.

Nathan must have heard me yelling because he began calling for me. I looked up toward him and saw him saying something. My hearing can be pretty bad sometimes, and I could not make out what he was trying to say.

"What was that?"

He attempted to tell me again. My guess is he was trying to be subtle about it since I was alone with the driver. Well, Bieko was there to but he was anxious to get his toy. Finally, Nathan reached into the manhole of the tanker, pulled out a bundle, and showed it to me. I immediately looked at the driver.

"Water, huh?"

The driver just stared at me with a look of defeat and was about to start speaking.

"Don't you dare say a fucking thing until I read you your rights. Then you can say whatever the hell you want!"

I reached for the mic of my radio and called out the code for narcotics. A few seconds later, a bunch of agents was running out of the checkpoint and making its way toward us. I rewarded Bieko with his toy and praised him for a while. He had done an awesome job and gotten us what would end up being our largest bust.

I continued to work with Bieko for two years. I was able to take him out a few times to the field and track groups in the brush. He was amazing out there, and thankfully, he never bit anyone we ever caught. I remember a few groups out there just chasing after him as I would let him get on scent and run. Agents like Santiago and Eliud would be out there with us, and we were all impressed with Bieko's abilities. The fact that about 95 percent of our time was spent at the checkpoint was still a drag for me, though. I couldn't shake it off and, after two years, was ready to let go of the leash.

A training officer position had opened up at our headquarters location, and I had applied for it. One day while on leave, I got a phone call from one of my canine supervisors letting me know that I had been selected for the training position and if I was still interested. I didn't hesitate at all. I informed him that I was interested and asked when I would start.

A week later, I said goodbye to Bieko and turned in my leash.

I had already been a field training officer (FTO) and was looking for the next step in my career. Not that I didn't enjoy what I was doing, but I think training others has been my greatest experience so far. Maybe not so much the fact of training others, I think it's more the entire aspect of sharing what I know with others. Sharing a different perspective or mind-set with other agents has always been a rewarding experience for me.

Prior to becoming an FTO, I asked some of the senior agents who had trained me when I first got to Falfurrias. My main concern was not being ready and ultimately being the cause of having mediocre agents working the field. The agents we train must be able to hold their own when working alongside our senior agents. Heck, they must be able to perform at all costs. One truly never knows when the shit will hit the fan and an agent is expected to react accordingly, regardless of whom we're working with.

I guess it's safe to say that I needed the "blessing" or validation from the agents who had trained me, agents like Rudy, Wiley, Ruben, Quicks, and Tali, to name a few. These guys had been instrumental during my "upbringing" in the patrol. If they could honestly tell me that I was ready to train others, then I would do it. Unfortunately for the trainees, all these guys said I was more than capable of training new agents.

I was partnered up with a female agent for a period of six months. During those six months, we trained two separate groups of agents. They didn't have it easy, and from everything that they keep telling me, I was a bit of an asshole to them during training. Okay, maybe more than a bit. The great thing about training others is that I had to place myself in check and be able to know all the material I was teaching them. I had to prepare myself for any possible questions they might have. The good thing about having a partner is that we could always bounce training ideas off each other and ultimately decide on the best approach for teaching a particular topic.

I, of course, had to blend my method of training with similar methods I used in the military. This meant that things would get fairly crazy and chaotic at times. I've always believed that, once you train an individual, the time will eventually come when you must test what they've learned. This would be more prevalent whenever we were training the new agents on how to track groups in the brush. Once they were given all the information they needed with regard to sign-cutting and tracking, they had to be left on their own so that they could actually apply that information. This way, they could figure out how to bridge the gaps between what they were seeing in the classroom environment and what was actually being seen out in the field.

There were some trainees who were slower than others, and different ways of training had to be utilized. We don't all learn things the same way. Some of them, okay, most of them, needed a bit more encouragement. This was always done through the effective use of colorful and tasteful vocabulary. Some mind games were also played from time to time just to keep the trainees on their toes. For example, at the end of every training week, Melissa and I would take all our trainees to a conference room. There, we would discuss everything that was learned throughout the course of the week. Now, because we didn't want the trainees to know exactly how well they were doing, we had to bash them up a little.

Some of the common phrases or sentiments used would be "You need to cowboy the fuck up!"

"Get your head out of your ass!"

"Quit being a suck ass, that won't get you anywhere with me!"

"I don't want to hear about what your daddy taught you! Your daddy is not here to train you, I am!"

"I need you to go home tonight and bitch-slap the shit out of your parents for fucking you up the way they did!"

And lastly, "I want you all to really think this weekend. Some of you need to consider changing careers. I feel I'm surrounded by morons!"

A senior agent and great mentor, El Dude, always had a great line: "How can I soar like an eagle when I'm surrounded by turkeys?" I have to admit that I've used it a few times throughout the years.

Most of those agents now tell me that they hated Fridays. They actually call them their bitch-session Fridays. They tell me how they used to go home every Friday wondering what the hell they were doing wrong. I was pretty good at making it seem as though they weren't doing a damn thing right. Little did they know, they were actually doing fairly well. I just didn't want them to know that, at least not so early in the training. They needed to remain open to new tactics and ideas. They needed to know that there is always something to be learned regardless of how good we get at our jobs. So if they went home thinking their methods in doing something had sucked, they would come in the following week thinking of how to improve those methods or of different ones to try out.

In the end, only the agents we trained and those who worked with them can answer whether or not our training method was any good. I think it was, and I believe that both our groups of trainees turned out pretty good. We can only train them; their personalities are their own.

This new gig that I had accepted was different, though. It is called postacademy training. During this training, agents continue to expand on all the material they learned while at the Border Patrol Academy. Only difference is, now during postacademy, we guide them and assist them in applying all that information on their fieldwork. I was partnered up with Alaniz for this particular endeavor, and it was a very productive three-year assignment.

When Alaniz and I first started, we were postacademy instructors only. At the end of our assignment, we had been allowed to actually oversee the sector's field training officer program, assist and teach portions of the senior agent or journeyman training, would assist in the certification of new instructors, and had been allowed to partake in the Border Patrol hiring boards and recruiting events. All these things were made possible through the guidance and direction of our supervisors, Fernie and Oscar. They never kept us from expanding our horizons and actually pushed for us to do more than what our duties entailed.

Covering the same material over and over with different groups can become a bit monotonous, so Alaniz and I had to figure out ways on how to make the classes more interesting. Sometimes, things just got amusing all on their own without us even trying. There were days when we would unknowingly create a funny situation, and then there were times when our trainees would either ask us something extremely outrageous or tell us about something funny that happened to them in the field. Heck, we even had a way of turning something serious into a joke or something to make fun of.

I remember one morning showing up at work feeling extremely tired. I had not gotten a good night's sleep and was feeling like crap, but I had to figure out a way to wake up because one of my classes was reviewing for an exam and I had to give them that review. So I stopped at a local gas station on my way to work and bought the largest energy drink I could find. When I got to the office that morning, I told Alaniz and our recruiter, Pete, about me not getting enough sleep and feeling like shit. The guys started laughing once they saw the huge energy drink in my hand.

About an hour into my review with the class, Pete and Alaniz came over to the classroom and offered me a preworkout pill. I didn't know much about those things at that time and surely didn't know what effect it might have on me. All I know is that the guys had said it could help me out if I was still feeling sluggish. I figured it wouldn't hurt and downed the pill with what was left of my energy drink. Man, was that a mistake.

An hour later, Alaniz walked back into the classroom to see if I needed help with the review. I didn't know at that time, but he had stood in the back of the room for a few minutes before I noticed him. I approached him to see if he needed something.

"Hey, bro, what's up?"

"Dude, what's up with you? You're all over the place."

"What? How am I all over the place?"

"Tinman, you're sitting down and standing back up every few seconds. You're speed-walking up and down the middle of the room in between slides, and you are talking fast as hell, man. Hell, I'm having a tough time keeping up with half of the shit you're saying."

"Really?"

"Yeah, man. Are you okay?"

"I feel a bit jittery, but otherwise I feel okay."

"Jittery?"

"Yeah, bro. I took that pill you and Pete gave me."

"Holy shit, Tinman. You took it with that energy drink? Dude, no wonder you're all over the place. Man, you're practically jumping off the walls!"

Alaniz told the class to take a break and then continued to laugh at my stupid ass. Hell, he even called Pete over and briefed him on everything I was doing. After a few laughs, I asked the class back in and continued with the review. I was able to control the jitters somehow and slowed down a bit so that the trainees could keep up with me and for the review to be effective. At the end of the day, the entire class passed the exam. I've never mixed a preworkout with an energy drink again.

We would hold formations every morning with our trainees, and then we would meet with them after formation just to touch base with everyone and see how things were going for them at their respective stations. I would mess with the trainees and with Alaniz sometimes by using old military tactics on them. I would wait for Alaniz to instruct a trainee to do something, and then I'd go to that trainee and pretend to be getting after him or her.

"You better not do what Mr. Alaniz told you to do. That shit is crazy. Hell, he's crazy; just look at him. He's got a crazy eye."

"Sir, I don't know; Mr. Alaniz told me to do this."

"Oh, so now Mr. Alaniz outranks me? Is this what you're telling me, trainee?"

"No, sir. I'm not saying that at all."

"Oh, so now I'm just hearing shit? Is that what you're saying? I'm the crazy one here, and I am just hearing shit! Are you calling me a liar, trainee?"

"No, sir. I'm not saying anything."

"Then you better sit your ass down and drive on with the last set of instructions given to you. You better not do what Mr. Alaniz said."

"Okay, sir."

I would wait a few minutes to ensure the trainee was not going to follow Alaniz's instructions, and then I'd go looking for Alaniz.

"Hey, bro. I thought you told that trainee to do something."

"I did, man. I wonder what's taking so long."

"Well, I just walked by the classroom, and the trainee is just sitting there talking to his classmates. The trainee decided to blow you off, bro. Damn trainee isn't doing shit you say."

Alaniz would normally lose his shit. Seeing him react was always priceless. I would always follow him as he would walk toward the trainee and demand to know what was taking so long. Then it would just become a game of who said what until I began laughing and all would be okay again.

Some of the other instructors who ended up working with us would chime in as well and always make fun of me whenever I was getting ready to address a group of trainees or senior agents. They would say that I would get way too serious on some of those speeches that they could actually see the US flag flapping behind me and a bald eagle land on my shoulder as I gave my speech or presentation.

Training was always fun, and I will venture to say that all of us learned a whole lot during our tenure in the department.

In Closing

....

After completing my assignment at the training department, I went back to my duty station, Falfurrias. Six months after that, I was able to get promoted to the rank of supervisory border patrol agent (SBPA). I had been trying for several years and was fortunate enough to finally get it. Being an SBPA also places a person in check. We must know our jobs and are expected to know all administrative functions that affect or are important to our agents. It is a huge responsibility to take on and should not be taken lightly. Once again, I find myself in a position where I can do more with regard to the patrol and be able to share my experiences and knowledge with others.

A year after my promotion, I was able to transfer to what is considered a Line Station. This new duty assignment placed me much closer to home and did away with the dreaded ninety-minute commute to work. Having worked at a checkpoint station for ten years made my transition fairly interesting. My new duty assignment's area of responsibility covers part of the actual Rio Grande River. Learning this aspect of my job has only continued to reinforce my opinion of possibly having one of the greatest jobs in the world. There is just so much that one can do within the patrol. The fear of having left or stopped working with a great group of agents in Falfurrias was unwarranted. I say this because I now continue my career alongside another great group of agents at my new station.

Sadly, I lost my mother shortly after starting my new assignment. Our relationship had been an estranged one for as long as I can remember. For one reason or another, my mom and I just never saw eye to eye on much of anything. She had demanded that I support her since the first day I left home and joined the military. I supported her until her last day. Maybe she felt it was my duty to do so since I was her only child and she never remarried. I did as expected. Unfortunately, I think this expectation led to our strained relationship. In the end, through thick and thin, I hope she knew I loved her dearly. She taught me so much in life, and for that, I am eternally grateful. I tell myself that she sacrificed our mother-and-son relationship by placing me in the care of my grandparents so that I could have a better life. I hope she was happy with the outcome and await the moment that I can ask her.

The past seven years have been a challenge. The few times I was ready to quit were rough. I could not have pushed through those times without the help of my wife. She is a wonderful woman. Thanks to her unwavering support and loving harassment, I went back to school and earned a master's degree in organizational management. She truly pushes me to be a better person.

Interestingly enough, my wife was also in the army. Although we didn't know each other while in service, we were both stationed at Fort Hood, Texas, at the same time. We were also stationed in Germany at the same time. Despite our serving in the same locations, we were in different units; and even then, she was probably the person I went to for any matters relating to my soldiers' or my own military pay since she worked at the finance offices that I had to report to for any issues. We definitely live in a small world. We were at the same locations for approximately six years, yet we wouldn't meet until after both of us had been honorably discharged from the army. She too continues her government service by working at a human resources department in a local Veterans Affairs office here in the Rio Grande Valley. We have a beautiful daughter who gets to reap all the benefits of our labor. I don't think she would say that things are easy for her since her parents are both military veterans, but hey, what do kids know nowadays?

I have seen ups and downs; I have taken lessons from both the good and the not so good. Plenty of mistakes have been made along the way, and I've tried to learn something from each of them. I have known whom to emulate and whom I do not want to become. I have interacted closely with so many different people and personalities throughout my life. I am fortunate enough to say that everybody who has left an impression has made me the person I am today.

I repeatedly tell people that we all learn from one another. The most junior person in the workplace can learn a lot from those with seniority and vice versa. We all bring something to the table; it's just a matter of figuring out what that "something" is. It's the finding out that makes the journey interesting.

There are times when I just sit outside in our patio by the grill with a cold drink in my hand. I look around me and just take everything in, relish the moment. What I've accomplished in life may not be much for a lot of people. That's okay; it's definitely more than enough for me. This in no way means that I am done. My pursuit in furthering my career continues, and my goal to learn from those around me seems to be endless.

So as I wait patiently for the new challenges that life and my career have in store for me, I take another sip of my cold drink, look at the US flag in my yard, and give thanks. I thank my parents for all they sacrificed so that I could have the opportunities I've had. I thank all those individuals who chose to take me under their wing and guide me to be a better soldier, agent, and person. I thank God for helping me push through all the dark times of my life and for the many blessings He has bestowed upon me.

I think back to where I started. I think back to those crop fields and the one dream I had as a kid. The dream to break the cycle of being a migrant worker. I look back at my time spent in the army and of the career I've had so far in the patrol. I remember all the great mentors I've had throughout my life: my parents, Chief Milyo, Staff Sergeant Dula, Arnold, El Dude, Wiley, Rudy, Ruben, Tali, Chief, Fernie, Oscar, Gene, and my wife. They, along with so many more, give me a sense of pride. The few things I've accomplished give me a sense of pride. My family gives me a sense of pride.

My flag, my country, my service—they are all reasons to be proud of. In the past and possibly even in the future, my upbringing and my roots have been questioned. They too are reasons to be proud of. I never forget where I started or where I come from. Aside from my wife and kids, my roots are a major part of my motivation.

From time to time, because of my job in the patrol, my nationality has been questioned. This will more than likely continue to happen. I don't understand why. Yes, I am of Mexican descent, but I am an American nonetheless.

While working at the checkpoint one day, an old white man came through the inspection lane I was on. When he stopped for his inspection, I walked toward the back of his pickup truck, looked through the back window, and visually inspected the entire vehicle. I didn't see anything that aroused any suspicion, and so I decided to keep my questions simple.

"Hello, sir, how are you today?"

"I'm fine, young man, can we move this along?"

"Sure thing, sir, mind telling me where you're headed?"

"I'm going home to San Antonio, not that it's any of your business."

I smiled and looked over at the canine handler who was working with me. He signaled that the vehicle was clear.

"Are you an American citizen, sir?"

The old man sighed out loud impatiently and gave me this look of utter disgust.

"Young man, I'm more American than you'll ever be!" One thought ran through my head immediately. Is this guy fucking serious?

I took a deep breath and decided to spend a few more seconds with the man and give him a bit of a history lesson with regard to my background.

"Maybe so, sir. Who's to say? May I ask you something else?"

"If it gets me out of here, go right ahead?"

"Did you ever serve in the military, sir?"

"No. I never had to."

"I never had to either, but I still served ten years of active duty in the army. I was also able to deploy during that time. I had to do and see things that I hope my kids never have to experience."

"Is that so?"

"Yes, sir. It is, and after ten years of military service, you now have me here wearing another green uniform, still serving my country. Funny thing is that I didn't have to do this either."

"So you see this as serving your country? How so?"

"Well, sir, you say that you live in San Antonio. Knowing that this checkpoint is here, who do you think will be questioned or looked at should a terrorist ever be encountered in your city? Do you think the media won't have a field day with us knowing that we are supposed to inspect every vehicle and person that comes through here? Would you not blame us or, should I say, me for not being able to arrest that individual?"

The old man didn't know what to say. He looked somewhat perplexed. "Young man. I mean, sir. May I please speak to your supervisor?"

After that question, I was puzzled. I reached for my radio mic and called for a supervisor. I then guided the old man to park his vehicle in the secondary inspection area so that he could be out of the inspection lane and be able to talk to my supervisor.

After a few moments, my supervisor called me over to the secondary area and had another agent cover my lane. I walked over not knowing what to expect.

"Yes, sir?"

The old man approached me and extended his hand for a handshake.

"Young man, I just want to apologize for being extremely rude with you. I've told your supervisor what a great job you're doing, and I wanted to personally thank you all for what you do."

Wow! I hadn't expected that outcome. I shook his hand, thanked him for his kind words, and wished him a safe trip home.

I guess the little lesson about my background and what we actually do in the patrol worked. If only it could work on everybody.

These are all just a few moments of my life that have made me the person I am today.

They are what make me a proud American.

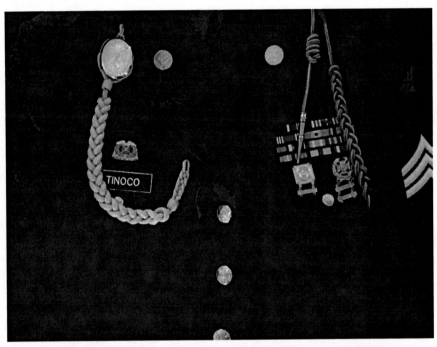

My encased uniform. My wife and daughter encased it for me
and placed it inside our office at home for my fortieth birthday.